THE CREATIVE BUREAUCRACY
& ITS RADICAL COMMON SENSE

BY CHARLES LANDRY
& MARGIE CAUST

COMEDIA

First published by Comedia in the UK in 2017

ISBN: 978-1-908777-08-9

Comedia The Round, Bournes Green Near Stroud, GL6 7NL, UK

Book design: **www.hillsdesign.co.uk**
All photographs: **Charles Landry**
Cover photograph: *Belfast City Hall*

Charles Landry has for 35 years attempted to shift how we think about the potential of cities and what their tangible and intangible resources can be starting with the concept of the Creative City in the late 1980's. This focuses on how cities can create the conditions to think, plan and act with imagination. Later he explored the sensory landscape of cities and how the art and science of cities can come together.

Margie Caust is based in Adelaide. She develops strategy and creates projects on city futures and the creative economy. Her main interest is finding value in areas that are often overlooked. Previously she was a civil servant in the UK and Australia working across multiple boundaries. She has an MSc in Urban Regeneration from UCL.

RECYCLED
Paper made from
recycled material
FSC
www.fsc.org   FSC® C007326

Printed on FSC® certified paper, using fully sustainable, vegetable oil-based inks, power from 100% renewable resources and waterless printing technology.

*Public offices with a
good atmosphere*

CONTENTS

*Following the path
in ICE Centre*

SUMMARY

Preface

Public bureaucracies across the globe face a converging, escalating crisis. Our societies are increasingly unequal. The population is ageing and they have fewer resources to respond to the growing need for care services. Demands for affordable living conditions are increasing as public space declines. Frenzied finance movements are rattling domestic economies. Mass migration is engendering fear and uncertainty. This accounts for some sudden and dangerous responses to overcome the effects of a turbo-charged capitalism. Add to this the rise in populism divides the world into 'patriots' and 'globalists' and is just a foretaste of what is to come. And overlaying everything our digitizing world and its disruptive technologies is providing both vast opportunities and threats.

There is a massive, urgent task ahead for bureaucracies to help create a fairer more equal world buttressed by an incentives and regulatory regime to match. They need to be smarter and cities need to be more creative as well, yet a city cannot achieve that if part of the system is uncreative.

There is a bigger context too, which is the demand by many to shift from representative democracy to participative citizenship and democracy. The rise of civic movements is a reflection of this and they are demanding more say in how decisions are made. All bureaucracies need to respond. Here the idea of the city as a commons or 'urban communing' jointly managed is gaining traction. It is a third way between public and private. This is creating stresses for some public institutions whilst others delight in it. It seeks to harness the energies of people and communities who wish to take more control over their lives and to improve facilities and services for all.

We are in the midst of redesigning the world and all its systems for 21st century conditions. Its principles should be **to bend the market to bigger picture purposes**. This needs a bureaucracy that can draw on all its ethical, creative and intellectual resources and reclaim a distinctive leadership role, but framed in a 21st century context.

Increasingly it is accepted that complex problems or deeper trends, areas we expect bureaucracies to lead on, will demand new ways of thinking and problem solving and especially the ability to partner and to connect across public, private and community divides.

Decades of reform have enfeebled bureaucracies, yet they have a reservoir of hidden potential

Decades of reform and challenge have enfeebled some parts of bureaucracies. Much of this change was to do with installing IT systems, automating processes that reduced human interaction and chopping departments around. The effect has been to fill officials with uncertainty and doubt about their legitimate role and authority relative to elected government. The pendulum has swung too far. Bureaucrats need to reclaim territory. To make this happen is less about technical innovations and more a shift in culture and social innovation.

We argue that:

• There is a reservoir of hidden potential and talent locked up in public bureaucracies. People can do much more if given the chance. This can unleash their discretionary effort. The desire to do more than you need to. But hard wired, rigid approaches within and across administrative systems, organizations, and individuals constrain what is possible.

• The inability to tap the creative agility of the bureaucracy to solve problems is wasteful. Digitization with its interactive opportunities can refresh our thinking to solve problems in new ways. And collaborating differently with communities can both reinvigorate democratic processes and the work experience.

• There is a direct link between the creativity of the bureaucracy and the success of a city. It's impossible to have an economically and socially successful city that is agile, attractive and sustainable without an inventive and engaged bureaucracy.

Our overall aim is to shift things **from a 'no, because' culture to a 'yes, if' culture** – one that captures possibilities and potential. This short book is targeted at those working in and outside bureaucracies. It seeks to inspire those inside the system and to shift perceptions of those outside who may have succumbed to knee jerk prejudices and clichés about who bureaucrats are, how they work and the potential of the public sector. Indeed, behind many great projects there is a creative bureaucrat, finding ways to shape the rules they operate with in positive directions.

We describe the features of a better bureaucracy and how it might be built and measured. We consider how individuals with agency can shift an organizational culture and, over time, even the bureaucratic system.

The ideas explored in the Creative Bureaucracy are drawn from many years working with and alongside people in the public sector. It draws too on numerous projects across the world to enhance the creative capacities of cities. It has benefitted from hundreds of conversations and interviews with bureaucrats and two longer term structured case studies in Bilbao and Adelaide.

The need for creativity is rising in all spheres of life. Public sector leaders agree it is a critical attribute for future leaders and staff at every level.[1] Yet their instincts favour risk management, risk aversion and compliance. The culture is hard to shift.

... almost universally bureaucrats want to contribute with more imagination

It is clear from our work that bureaucrats almost universally want to contribute more imaginatively. Most feel underutilised and stymied into expressing themselves narrowly. Yet things are beginning to break out. Some are being inspired by new ways of working. Innovative initiatives and experimental bureaucratic cultures are on the rise across the globe, even if mostly on the edges. Some changes are being forced by citizens who want to shift the atmosphere of their cities and are prepared to defy rules to do so. In other cases, it is business who is leading the charge.

So **what is preventing the bureaucracy from embracing the potential of bureaucrats?** Where are there signs of breaking out? And can individuals influence the potential of bureaucracies and its systems?

In the Creative Bureaucracy we explore these ideas primarily through the lens of the 'lived experience' of bureaucrats. Here we find examples of heroic courage but also of misery. Our time needs the energy of inventive bureaucrats prepared to tackle the big and small issues we face.

Creative bureaucrats can, as individuals, shape cities. But a critical mass can reshape the bureaucratic system itself. Organizations can then embody the values and qualities expressed by the best individuals. This can humanise organizations and bring forth new energies and talents from employees. We explore the pressures on individuals, organizations and systems to move forward from the era of restrictive managerialism that often ignores the bigger social change trends happening outside the organization. A result, ideally, would be **to trigger a movement of bureaucrats who demand more from their work** environments.

Bureaucracies shape and influence cities, particularly their 'atmosphere', the intangible but nevertheless real experience that can encourage or discourage entrepreneurs and citizens. We draw on examples from different bureaucracies to build in engagement, innovation and to project a generosity of spirit. This civic creativity can help communities bridge divides and find 'the common' in our quest to build better places to live.

Setting the scene

'Creativity' and 'bureaucracy' are two words apparently in tension. The creative bureaucracy thesis seeks to marry these two seemingly incompatible concepts. Creativity focuses on resourcefulness, imagination, responsiveness, adaptability and flexibility. Say the word 'bureaucracy' to yourself. What does it conjure up? Mindless rules, lazy complacency, incomprehensible forms, red tape, inefficient, convoluted, overpaid, wasting resources – a string of negative connotations with few redeeming qualities. This is not the full story. The very things bureaucracy is criticised for are also insurances against the abuse of power. Here we mostly use the word 'bureaucracy' rather than administration advisedly for two reasons.

They are both to startle and to provoke so that readers might think afresh. We want to recapture the common good as a positive virtue and those working in public service are often its good defenders. So whilst we criticize many workings of most current bureaucracies and their need to tap into the commitment and energy of citizens, younger start-ups or established businesses, especially those that value the public good, we are seeking to describe a new one fit for the ethos, the conditions, and needs of now and tomorrow.

The standardised rules, hierarchies and procedures of a bureaucracy were designed to be positive, or at least efficient and fair. Bureaucracies were developed to solve the problems of their time and so reflect the culture of their age. These cultures were more deferential, more top down and hierarchical, more expert driven, less emotionally intelligent. At their best they sought systematic procedures to bring transparency, fairness and equity to decision making. They were once seen as benign and modern, if somewhat technocratic. Yet as they evolved, weaknesses appeared. Problem solving seemed mechanical and planning ahead seemed achievable in a 'predict and provide' fashion. Today by contrast we need a form of **elastic planning that is strategically principled and tactically flexible**.

In a world of wicked, interconnected problems and a complex risk nexus the older approach is at best sub-optimal and at worst dysfunctional. Today you can only strive for better rather than perfect outcomes. Nudging at a problem or adapting to new circumstances and dynamics become important but so does the occasional radical re-assessment.[2]

Spandau: City Hall and its citizen's office. Today the architecture would be more transparent

There is, we believe, a bureaucratic model fit for the challenges of the 21st century. It will not be the same as what went before. It will use the best of digital potentials, but will not let technologies dehumanize developments. Its 'modus operandi' will be to stimulate and enliven itself and its environment by drawing on the potential of its people and through a more co-creative, equal exchange with its communities of interest.

Exploring bureaucratic change

We are not the first to explore the dilemmas of bureaucracy, but our focus on the lived experience of the bureaucrat and the bureaucracy's internal life is different and novel. There is a vast literature on the attempts to address the systemic problems of bureaucratic effectiveness or innovations in governance both in public and private organizations. This literature has grown exponentially. There are many organizations, too, trying to revisit the bureaucratic model coming from varied directions. Yet we have discovered none that looks at the issues from the perspective of the individual bureaucrat and their human potential. Nor is there a focus on emotional intelligence, which acknowledges equality across roles, and clearly a shared culture, and a joint mission. It is this that triggers the discretionary effort.

Think tanks, university programmes and researchers, government hybrids or supranational organizations focusing on public sector innovation have reached broadly similar conclusions about good performance, effectiveness and creativity. It includes leaderships that empower, strategic focus and the human centred use of IT systems.

Berlin: Play on German word Müll (garbage). Garbage collectors are multi-talented

Below we give a snapshot of this increasingly rich landscape that readers can follow up. They include global organizations like OECD and its Observatory of Public Sector Innovation, which focuses on establishing rules and processes that foster innovation as well as breaking discipline boundaries[3]; semi-governmental organizations like MindLab, in Copenhagen[4] a cross-governmental innovation unit that involves citizens and businesses in creating new solutions for society. It is also a physical space or neutral zone that seeks to inspire innovation and collaboration.

... increasingly attention is being paid to bureaucratic innovation

There is Change@SA[5] in Adelaide, which seeks to create a culture of collaboration, continual improvement and inventiveness within a vibrant public service; semi-independent city hall based labs like Lab para la Cuidad in Mexico City,[6] which seeks to connect citizens and the city in novel ways by using the megalopolis as a proving ground; there is the Urban Lab in Paris[7] with its focus on experimenting with climate change solutions; universities such as the Ash Center for Democratic Governance & Innovation at Harvard[8] whose project on municipal innovation supports the replication and adaptation of good practices working closely with local officials.

A new range of think tanks is emerging like Kennisland in Amsterdam[9], which starts with the users of public services to assess whether they connect with real needs and what citizens could do themselves. On the government side they have set up customized learning platforms to help solve the problems of public organizations and individual professionals such as with the Slimmernetwerk (Smarter Network). Attached to this is the Doetank (Do-tank) whose aim is learning by doing in helping public servants innovate themselves. Another network is the Kafka Brigade[10] an international research group 'on red tape and dysfunctional bureaucracy'. It addresses what to do when citizens and public servants become tangled in a web of too complex procedures. Kafka Brigades bring together all parties from front line workers, managers and policymakers around particular cases, such as revising domestic abuse procedures, rethinking support for 18-24 year olds seeking work or how to overcome the barriers for green growth.

NESTA[11] in London, now a charitable body was set up by a government endowment and seeks to be: 'an innovation foundation... we back new ideas to tackle the big challenges of our time'. Such as how to use digital tools to improve the quality and legitimacy of decision-making or helping create the 'Second Half Fund' that supports the growth of innovations that mobilise the time and talents of older people to help others alongside public services, such as becoming volunteer teachers in schools.

... the older bureaucratic model needs rethinking

All these entities have similar aims, namely collaborative problem solving, engaging citizens in new ways or breaking down older organizational paradigms. Collectively their methods and approaches stress openness and a willingness to re-assess assumptions, a focus on social innovation as a catalyst of change, **fostering an experimentation culture** centred perhaps on living labs, rethinking issues like procurement, embracing measured risks and unleashing the capacities of individuals who bring forth a form of 'bureaucratic creativity' capable of transforming organizations and systems. Crucially they highlight the need for real life experiments that, if they work well, become common practice.

KANALISATION
· VON ·
· BERLIN ·
RADIALSYSTEM · V
· * ·
· ERWEITERT ·
· A·D·1904·05 ·

A HUMANE SYSTEM

Feeling fulfilled

There are urgent concerns about work environments. People are more unhappy than happy at work. This is a long-term trend and for many this leads people to be disengaged and to under-perform. The so-called 'creativity gap' identified by Adobe in its global survey of 5000 people 'State of Create' (2016)[12], highlights how peoples' potential is under-explored. Only 31% believe they are living up to their creative potential.

Engaged employees and managers are more creative, passionate and productive. They bring life and energy to an organization as a free gift and resource.

Private sector organizations don't engage their employees well, in spite of evidence that it increases financial performance, but public sector and government organizations may be worse. This failure to engage employees has many consequences: for them as individuals, for the problem solving and emotional climate of bureaucracies; and for the cities and regions in which they are located. With change accelerating across all domains of society, public institutions are falling further behind.

We have seen and experienced many wonderful examples of the effectiveness of the public sector. But the intense, visceral frustration and emotional pain experienced by some of the best minds in public service cannot be over-stated. **Too many people feel reduced at work, they cannot give of their best** and so energies are used elsewhere in their private worlds or in distractions.

This is why we are interested in the 'creative bureaucracy' and whether it can mirror peoples' internal sense of who they are and match the aspirations they have for their life. Charles as an outsider has observed the bureaucracy at work and Margie as an insider has lived the bureaucratic experience. For nearly three decades both have been working with or within public institutions in cities and regions across the world as well as with their leaders, their administrations, local community groups and business

Berlin: Radialsystem – A Space for Arts & Ideas in former pumping station. A creative bureaucrat Jutta Weitz helped make it happen

and creative sectors as they attempt to adapt and respond to the massive changes confronting them.

Regardless of the country or city, the administrative logic and character of government systems or organizational purpose is shared: silos; a lack of integrated and holistic thinking; an inability to cross boundaries; reluctance to see the benefits of interdisciplinary working and unwillingness to truly partner or to connect imaginatively with outside worlds - in spite of these things having been highlighted for 25 years.

Across the world there has been a **whittling away of policy imagination** and big thinking. Often the most interesting work is outsourced to 'think tanks', consultants or to 'innovation teams'. People in the system feel stymied and curtailed. It engenders a negative mood. A blame culture then breeds fearfulness. It is when organizations together from their differing important perspectives work on joint problems, that often the best solutions emerge.

People say 'the inertia is immense' and 'it's the rigidity, I can't bear it', and the 'inflexibility, that does not allow you respond effectively'. 'All I know is that some of the best people are leaving', and 'we find it hard to hold on to the young and enthusiastic, they start with energy and then feel drained as they bump into barriers'. 'It is difficult to appoint the best or get the worst to leave'. 'The lack of organizational emotion cannot inspire staff. The atmosphere needs to be 'warm' to develop an R&D culture'. 'The environment of risk aversion does not understand the difference between risk and uncertainty'. **'I wanted a 'yes', but it is so much easier to say 'no'.**

There are costs, we have concluded, of not having a more creative bureaucracy. The first cost is **wasted human potential**. There is a reservoir of hidden potential and talent locked up in public bureaucracies.

Frightening statistics tell a story about disengagement and under achievement at work. Gallup, for instance, for over 15 years in the US, has measured employee engagement in public and private workplaces covering several million respondents. The research concludes that only around 32% of the US workforce are engaged and inspired by what they do. Nearly 70% are emotionally disconnected. 50% of these are 'disengaged' 'just kind of present, but not inspired by their work or their managers'. Nearly 20% are 'actively disengaged' as they 'have bosses from hell that make them miserable, and so roam the halls spreading discontent'.[13] Even worse, the worldwide survey has found that only 13% of the global workforce is actively engaged.[14] There were strong country differences with the USA and Canada scoring most highly with 29% engaged, 54% disengaged and 18% actively disengaged. For Western Europe the figures were 14% engaged, 66% disengaged and 20% actively disengaged. The worst figures were for East Asia with 6%, 68% and 26% respectively.

Our own longer-term structured interview series of several hundred diverse national, regional and city government officials in over 25 cities from Bilbao, to Adelaide, Helsinki and Taipei as part of our Creative City Index work revealed similar results. On average people work at only 65% capacity. They tell us they could do 35% more if their operating environment were different. Good managers, leaders and committed staff overwork themselves, operating at 120% capacity and often at the edge of burnout in order to make 'the system' work.

The second cost is **the inability to tap the creative agility** of the bureaucracy to solve problems. Dramatic pressures are demanding change. The context is ever-increasing demands, ever-reducing budgets and short-term thinking governed by electoral cycles. Yet digitization with its new platforms and technologies are opportunities to think about problems in new ways. These interactive opportunities can refresh democracy, but most bureaucracies do not yet know how to use them.

You can't be a creative city without a creative bureaucracy

The third cost is **to the city, region or nation** as prospects leech away, motivation is drained and the talented move elsewhere. Bureaucracies unable to mobilise and harness their own collective imagination and potential are unlikely to make the most of their city's assets. An engaged bureaucracy can lift the local environment. A disengaged one can depress opportunities as they affect the atmosphere of a city, shaping the way it feels.

The link between the creativity of the bureaucracy and the success of the city is direct and strong. Cities cannot be comprehensibly successful, alert, agile, attractive and sustainable without an imaginative and engaged bureaucracy.

Carol Ryff summarizes[15] well the qualities we need to make us feel fulfilled. She outlines six measures that provide people with the sense of psychological stability, ease about themselves and being human. How well do most bureaucracies do in achieving this? They are: how people are making use of their personal talents and potential (personal growth); the depth of connection they have in ties with significant others (positive relationships); whether they view themselves to be living in accord with their own personal convictions, in essence being themselves (autonomy); how well they are managing their life situations (environmental mastery); the extent to which people feel their lives have meaning, purpose, and direction (purpose in life); and the knowledge and acceptance they have of themselves, including awareness of personal limitations (self-acceptance).

Highlighting the human perspective

'The Creative Bureaucracy' understands that people are at the heart of the system. It puts the human perspective and the lived experience of working within or with a bureaucracy centre-stage. A bureaucracy, crucially, is not only a structure and an 'organigram' with functional relationships and roles. It is a group of people with lives, emotions, aspirations, energy, passion and values. To adapt Shakespeare's famous quote: 'What is the bureaucracy, but the people in it?'

Most of those we have spoken to tell us that they work in the bureaucracy because they want to make a difference in the world. In big and small ways they see their work as meaningful. It's just that the context is frustrating.

Bureaucrats often have strong principles, great intentions and good ideas. Most want to do good. We are not naïve to the complexities of working lives in organizations. There are 'pen pushers' as in commercial organizations. Add to this brew the human frailties of power play, factionalism, individualism, egotism, micro-politics, jealousy or blatant resistance. But is the individual at fault or dysfunctional organizations or systems? Humane systems bring out peoples' better selves.

Who is this bureaucrat? They are not automatons. It is the head of a department, the assistant fire officer, the teacher, the youth worker, the district nurse, or planning manager, someone who protects the environment, the parking attendant, the cultural programme manager, the business development officer, the CEO. We are interested in the contribution bureaucrats can make at all levels – senior leaders, middle management and those with more routine tasks.

Bureaucracies are beginning to transform... Their energy is ready to be tapped

We ask: Is there an inner logic to all organizations across cultures and time that constrains and reduces people? Or can we think afresh?

Bureaucracies are beginning to transform. We are optimistic about the positive changes on the horizon. We know of bureaucrats across the world, attempting to rethink possibilities. It is easy to emphasise negative working experiences and many feel frustrated. Yet many, if not most, long to be engaged in real ways. Their energy is ready to be tapped. People mostly were initially drawn to working in the bureaucracy because of shared values. Working in a bureaucracy that allows people to express these values triggers their desire to contribute. The challenge is to create the conditions in which they can. Crucially, many in their private lives are part of interesting civic organizations or platforms and know there are other ways of working.

Harnessing the discretionary effort

Bureaucracies created solely in pursuit of efficiency are extraordinarily wasteful of human effort and talent. A creative one, by contrast, engages people so that they extend their potential and build their energy. This unleashes the discretionary effort the unrealised resource that can make organizations more or less successful.

Every individual has a vast storehouse of "discretionary" effort that they either give or withhold on a daily basis. Discretionary effort is the difference between how people are capable of performing and how well they actually perform. It's both in the power of employees and a factor of systems that can encourage or prevent people making contributions. Studies, including our own in various cities, show that when people do not feel aligned to the organizational mission and/or culture, the organization can lose between 30% to 50% of their potential contribution. Instead of performing more strongly, having ideas, solving problems, making the work environment better, helping others out, they are potentially frustrated, bored, stressed or close themselves in.

What is required to entice individuals to give this extra effort? It is a mix of things both general and specific: a positive, respectful atmosphere; an ethos that sharing and helping out is good and it will be reciprocated; creating excitement about a project, a target or a goal; people need to feel they have agency; stressing how everyone counts and that their contribution matters and has an impact; ensuring they are identified with the outcome and praised; providing an incentive, a reward or a personal gain; perhaps personalizing a challenge and helping you do give of your best. In addition it involves creating a culture where slacking and task avoiding feels wrong. An emotionally strong organization will seek to understand the motivations of those and try to get them to switch so they might contribute to the team. Slackers deflate an organization.

Discretionary effort is the unrealised resource

This goes beyond simplistic notions around management systems. Fundamental is an attitude of leadership that sees the organization as a joint endeavour where everyone is essential and where everyone can learn and everyone teach. This requires systems that allow rather than curtail and that create a dynamic which leverages strengths. Most studies say this involves widespread leadership rather than management. Systems are managed; people are led. Everyone can play a leadership role. Here leadership is defined as a relationship, rather than a position, so it is behaviour based. Self-awareness and empathy are key components in the relationship's success.

The emotional organization

The best work often happens in a spirit of play but most organizations expect people to be serious. It's inevitable that work elicits our full range of emotions. But employees are expected to operate almost without emotion, as if 'the system' were a lifeless being. Emotions are our source of energy.

Startling under-explored **facts about people feeling alienated, even distressed, are largely missing** in global discussions of innovation especially related to the public sector, our focus here. Working within a 'system' can feel qualitatively different to working in, say, a start-up. A system can feel pervasive. You can see it in the worn down, drained faces of people who have been 'in the system' too long. They are going through the motions. But others refuse to surrender. They rebel. They count victories in small advances.

Contrast that with Clemens Muecke, head of economic development in Neukölln, a relatively poor but changing district in Berlin. 41 years working for the authority, he looks fresh as he feels he has agency in helping to make things happen – less concerned about being the overall boss and more about getting results. He helped negotiate the success of the emblematic Klunkerkranich Club sited on a carpark roof of a shopping centre. Its atmosphere changes throughout the day, mothers and kids earlier on in the day and increasingly a techno club as the evening nears. The roof garden is cared for by 20 volunteers and no flowers are damaged as the rave crowd comes in. Locals enter for free. It balances well the locals and the nomads. To make this happen needed a connector between founders Robin, Dorle and Julian and the various wings of the authority. This was Clemens and his example focuses on agency.

The ability for people to have a sense of agency is crucial

The emotionally intelligent organization understands the differing motivations of people and helps foster their ability and their sense of agency. This is the capacity of people to act independently and to make their own free choices. Too much structure by contrast shapes, confines or limits this possibility. There is always a balancing act between agency and structure as the latter embeds the organization's ethos and goals. Clemens has been able to act

as he is trusted. In general the balance needs to shift to give individuals more say just as they ideally have in their personal lives. People need to feel and act out the full person they can be at work.[16]

Contorting creativity

'Behind every great project is a creative bureaucrat' and 'they are mostly invisible and unacknowledged' so exclaimed Jochen Sandig founder of Radialsystem in Berlin, responding to a creative bureaucracy workshop. This is a large space for the arts and ideas located in a former pumping station with a waterside terrace. He was referring to Jutta Weitz, responsible for allocating industrial sites in the city in a period of transition and who promoted Zwischennutzung (transitional uses). Jochen claimed she really made things happen. She negotiated him and his team through the bureaucratic complexities of licenses and navigated them through the minefield of rules, how to phrase an application, how to describe a budget, and when to push and when to hold back.

The quiet and unassuming Jair Lin as the number two in urban planning in Taipei, understood the subtle ecology of how creative milieux work. He knew how to 'bend' the market and create rules to both encourage young start-ups as well as rescue the traditional Dihua St. area in Dadaocheng. His Urban Regeneration Office (URO) was open to experiments. It connected with progressive developers and sought to control the development of key small sites such as to contain the speculative dynamism present in the city. One strategy was to transfer some property rights in exchange for keeping the original buildings.

The Athens Vice-Mayor for Civil Society Amalia Zepou, formerly a documentary filmmaker, created the platform "synAthina" to trigger a new energetic relationship between citizens and the public domain. This was more than voluntarism, but a co-creative process of active citizenship and an open minded administration. It developed into an idea that won one of the five Mayors' Challenge awards from Bloomberg Philanthropies in 2014. SynAthina is now part of a social innovation unit, a systematic mechanism between the municipality, local organizations and citizens. The aim is to facilitate citizens' creativity to modernise local governance to improve citizens' lives and strengthen the democratic process. An example is 'atenistas' a group of imaginative people with no legal entity. In 2010, they had the idea of covering abandoned historical buildings in Athens with paper banners on which they wrote the buildings' history. In 2013, the synAthina network managed to find a sponsor to print the text on small discreet plexiglass banners for 15 buildings in the city centre.

This was in theory not allowed and the 'defining moment' was how both the municipality legal service and the technical services changed the regulation and facilitated permissions for placing banners. They adopted the idea as a municipal service and then expanded it to more buildings. Instead of the usual negative response, city officials are now more open to new practices. That is culture change.

Many people are waiting in the wings to contribute more

The people mentioned above are exceptional. But many more are waiting in the wings. Qualities of inventiveness are less embedded, legitimized or encouraged in public entities. Yet these energies spill over and burst out. Imagination sometimes has to be expressed in convoluted ways to make an impact. In essence bureaucratic creativity is about finding solutions by overcoming obstacles to intractable problems or discovering fresh opportunities.

The scope and form of bureaucratic ingenuity is shaped by its context. We see it more as resourcefulness and do not give it the name – creativity. Yet it is the creativity of wriggling around departmental obstacles. The creativity of knowing where and when to pitch an idea. The creativity of claiming a leftover budget.

The ability to redefine a project so it fits a funding stream. The fine sense to know when to push and when to hold back or when to leave things obscure. In short, knowing how to get your way whilst working within limitations.

This is not the creativity of the artist, the clever entrepreneur or social enterprise. These often, can boldly go with the flow of an idea, can come across as fresh and alert, can invent, can feel they can be themselves, can be named or acknowledged. For bureaucrats a kind of thwarted creativity bursts out at times with the energy of the contortionist, and the creativity of helping others achieve their aims. A more open bureaucratic system would allow officials to be imaginative as a matter of course.

Imagining civic creativity

In the 1990s 'The Creative City' highlighted the urgency of civic creativity and to quote we said: *'Civic creativity' is defined as imaginative problem-solving applied to public good objectives. The aim is to generate a continual flow of innovative solutions to problems which have an impact on the public realm. 'Civic creativity' is the capacity for public officials, businesses, large and small, or civil society organizations together to effectively and instrumentally apply their imaginative faculties... this agenda seeks to be a means and guiding principle to make this happen'.*[17]

> Creativity focused on public interest aims is a central task for our age

The creative bureaucrat is the (often) invisible guide behind civic creativity. Their efforts, in combination, result in this new value driven organizational form and they are adaptive, responsive, flexible, collaborative and outward looking. They encourage others to be both solid in executing tasks that inevitably can be routine, yet also imaginative and inventive. They connect people at a humane level at work and create the conditions needed for openness and creativity to emerge. If they are sufficiently influential, they transform their organizations which embody their values. The organization then makes better places or cities by the ways it works internally and with outsiders. Indeed the physical look, feel and atmosphere of cities can exude this ethos and spirit.

This 'creative bureaucracy' is not just a fixed entity unto itself. It is in a dynamic relationship with its people and with the city, the citizens and the world in which it sits. It allows for honesty, a lack of defensiveness, a listening ethos and trialling and testing approach that sharpens programmes and projects.

NESTA[18] describes this as an 'innovative adhocracy'. This is essentially a knowledge-intensive organization that operates more organically internally and with great flexibility.

Most bureaucrats walk a fine line. **Arbitrary creativity can appear risky or be simply fluffy**. The context is all important. An organization has a purpose and values and is usually governed by legislation and policy. This governs its ethics and the conduct of people who work there and how they and the organization relates to the outside world. Public sector creativity focused on public goods is special – it is a form of civic creativity.

The creativity of the public sector will differ from that of an independent start-up, a corporate or NGO. The concept of 'civic creativity' is important and again brings together two words that do not seem to connect. 'Civic' sounds worthy, staid and somewhat uninspiring. 'Creative' still has a vibrant, energetic ring to it. In combination the idea can exude potential.

Dissolving, resolving and harnessing the ambiguity and tension between these two opposites lies at the heart of 'civic creativity'. Imaginative problem solving or creating opportunities can enhance the public good and provide better services. It involves using the diverse energies, skills and values of the public, private and community sectors

and getting them to talk and work together to achieve mutually satisfactory results.

This can be difficult. The aims of one often frustrate and hinder those of the other. They may have opposing objectives or organizational cultures. One might want to maximize their personal returns, and be concerned only with their project in isolation, rarely looking at how it fits into the wider urban picture; the other might focus on public realm benefits; and the third may want to maintain a sense of locality and authenticity that comes from leaving things as they are.

Consider, for instance, the great places you love and you will see a fine and gratifying blend of the non-commercial and commercial, the locally authentic and globally oriented or inspirational and the ordinary.

The balance between these aspects will have been hard fought. There will be a backstory of wrangling and argument where one sought to dominate the other. Somewhere in all of this will have been some creative bureaucrats capable of drawing together, contorting possibilities, and somehow getting things right in the context of difficult odds.

Atmosphere and mood

Adelaide: The interesting Commonwealth Law Courts was easier to build as the federal government controlled the land and planning

A successful blend of 'civic' and 'creativity' creates an atmosphere that inspires people to trust their own creative impulses. The mood of a city is much more shaped by the actions, big and small, of public entities than we think. A substantial literature exists on what makes a city feel like a place you'd like to live or work in or why some cities are magnets and why others leak talent.

Civic generosity is a powerful resource and the pay-back is astonishing

Citizens or businesses, of course, help create the atmosphere, but imagine all the ways that government employees influence the mood of the city. If there is 'civic generosity', it has a powerful impact. Too little is written about this. The officer at immigration can avoid your eyes, look bored and even intimidating. Or they can smile; welcome you to their country and invite you to enjoy your stay.

The design of the streets can signal a place that prefers cars and moving fast. Or enlightened city planners and elected councillors can have collaborated to make the city a place for pedestrians, with green spaces, easy for children and the disabled to navigate, well-lit and inviting.

Your local council office can treat you like a number as you grab a ticket and wait to be served, or it can help you feel like a valued citizen. Your local hospital can make you stand and queue and wait your turn, increasing your sense of vulnerability and powerlessness, or they can invite you to be comfortable and come to you, interested and concerned about your situation.

Police officers can aim to intimidate or they can aim to calm and reassure. Bureaucrats can take an attitude of 'you've got the wrong number it's not my problem' or they can express interest and even take action.

Every day we have multiple interactions with public entities, even if we do so through the results of their policies and programmes. And there have been positive changes. Speaking to the tax office in most European countries is now no longer a frightening chore, even though you may have to go through a robotic process to reach a human being.

The atmosphere a bureaucracy creates shapes how a city feels

Most importantly bureaucracies across the States, some parts of Europe and to the East have begun to loosen up. This has allowed new voices to be heard. Cities now feel more like a shared endeavour. The atmosphere is changing. Rights and responsibilities are shifting. Bureaucracies and citizens are creating the mood together with the latter taking more control or creating new platforms or horizontal connections, independent of government.

This reclaiming of power can be seen, most firmly, in rising political protest movements or tactical urbanism.[19] Projects such as 'parking day', 'restaurant day', 'better block' or 'guerrilla gardening' or 'cleaning day' stem from the same ethos. Citizens can unite even if they never meet physically.

The open data movement is another expression. This has unleashed a plethora of app driven solutions to help make cities work better. City Mapper creates a refined picture of how citizens can move around the city. Garbage bins can communicate when they are full. Helsinki Region Infoshare[20] is an example of an enabling mechanism where people can play with data in a way that fosters entrepreneurship. Here for the first time in history the young are better equipped, as digital natives, than the old 'digital settlers', to deal with the substantial cultural implications of this power shift.

Historically, community responsibility and its problems were 'outsourced' to the public administration, which was a service production engine. That era had its mood. It felt more top down. You could hear refrains, such as: 'why does the city not clean the streets', 'why does it not solve the problem of noisy young people' or 'why are the trains not arriving on time'.

Yet change is inevitable. The challenge of the era is to find ways to mobilise human potential. When the aim is to redefine the city and its component parts, including its bureaucracies, as a 'community of brains', a different paradigm and value set emerges. When the city is no longer a set of mostly physical infrastructures, the aim becomes to harness the collective goodwill and community intelligence. This can be brought out or held back and here the more open bureaucracy helps the former.

... Our major resource is human potential and this needs to be mobilized

Here the city and citizens communicate with each other differently, without stressing 'who's in charge'. They are the radical civics in action as Amalia Zepou in Athens shows.[21] We are only at the beginning as these challenges to traditional notions of democracy or public sector organization unfold. The combination of principle and technology has made working transparently with more shared control possible. The communications revolution has broken the monopoly of the public sector. This may be a blessing.

So power is shifting with **more ways for people to connect with the like-minded**. Some bureaucracies are embracing the potential, one thinks here of Amsterdam, Athens or Torino, acting more as platforms to connect opportunity. In this context the creative bureaucrat is able to enable and respond, to sense the atmosphere, but not control. They are driven to explore and experiment - while being ready to adjust to changing conditions.

Added together these small examples and big and the attitudes underlying them reflect what we call a humane system.

They expect to translate this sense of 'agency' across all aspects of their lives.

WE LIVE
IN A RAINBOW
OF CHAOS

FITTING INTO A SHIFTING LANDSCAPE

The context for the bureaucracy is shifting and that landscape requires the new operating system. In a digitalised world individuals command systems and technology and use them to shape their own lives.

Command and control systems no longer work. As public bureaucracies change so too will the outside world's view of what they can offer to society if they are able to operate at their best. It has been too easy to scapegoat the bureaucracy. But we are living unprecedented times and how we navigate them will depend on how agile, inventive, and respected bureaucracies manage to become. Bureaucracies need to feel confident in their legitimacy, but in a 21st century form.

Converging & unpredictable megatrends

Profound shifts, changes, disruptive technologies and political re-alignments are reshaping expectations or potential, such as where and how we live, and how we want the world to work. Megatrends such as urbanisation, living together in harmony, populism, climate change, globalisation and technology are complex, interconnected and converging. And in addition we, as Roy Amara[22] notes, 'tend to overestimate the effect of a technology in the short run and underestimate the effect in the long run'.

There are no 'off the shelf' solutions. Wicked problems are proliferating; these are problems we must address even though we do not know the precise answer or roadmaps. This calls for foresight and the ability to relax into uncertainty or ambiguity as we invent the future. Stark and threatening choices face humanity and although we know what a richer, sustainable life could be, our collective intelligence seems incapable of making it happen.

Governments, across all levels, especially through their convening power and in collaboration with others, are called upon to provide the guidance, roadmaps and programmes that will anticipate and avert looming catastrophes, grow the quality of life, reduce inequalities and stimulate economies. Here government refers to elected government and their linked teams and to their

Miami: A graffiti encapsulates the choices we have to make

'administrations'. Bureaucracies enact and deliver national and local government policy and programmes. Each needs foresight, imagination and agility to respond to what lies ahead. And most importantly they need an ethical framework to guide their actions.

Bureaucracies on the back foot

The public bureaucracy can play a crucial role, with others, in making the best of opportunities but only if it reinvents itself in terms of its democratic processes, its moral system or, crucially, its way of operating. It has fallen behind other sectors, such as business or social life regarding their organizational forms and operating methods. Yet the world outside of the bureaucracy needs to recognize its value and values too. The rise of civic movements is one example.

... Bureaucracies are behind other sectors in re-assessing their organizational forms

Many years of reform and continued questioning of their roles and competences have drained bureaucracies of their confidence. The anonymous bureaucracy has become a scapegoat for broader discontents. It often encapsulates frustrations that have nothing specifically to do with public administrations. It has made them uncertain about how to act.

The public sector has been on the defensive and has not been able to give credence to its public interest or common good concerns. Let us remember the good reasons for bureaucracy and their post-Enlightenment origins, which were to create fairness, equity, equality of opportunity, due process and transparency. These are important achievements of democracy and need to be maintained to avoid special interests dominating society or corruption. Yet now these virtues are seen to stifle and to slow things down.

Now new, often negative, political forces may also reduce the potential of the bureaucracy to provide stability or to act with legitimacy.

Managerialism drains confidence

In the last few decades it has been argued that bureaucracies can be managed as though they are private companies even though their purposes and criteria for success are different.

The system started to change through a combination of adopting private sector management techniques, building up of special offices and the advisor culture, and the reduction in some jurisdictions of tenure for civil servants and downgrading policy units. These have gone out of favour and been a source of easy savings and often disappeared. They have sometimes been replaced with reform units or innovation functions. Forward, insightful thinking can then be lost.

This all weakened the bureaucracy and stymied them, so adding to a sense of being disempowered and stuck. In some places, heads of big departments effectively became chief executives who relied on the favour of a minister or a mayor to retain their positions. The will of ministers could be expressed too through a range of politically appointed advisors who often wield great power and influence.

Public administrations across the world have **not been able to resist the rise of the new managerialism**. The resulting efficiency paradigms have partly been beneficial in reshaping how bureaucracies operate. They have become more accountable to their publics. But there are negatives. One consequence is the overweening box-ticking or checking mentality. Another is technology being projected as the saviour with the proliferation of automated systems that feel robotic. Or decisions made by algorithms that fail the test for common sense with services unable to respond to individual circumstances.

Managerialism ceaselessly pushes an approach whereby all human affairs are driven by instrumental rationality. The most cost-effective means to achieve things always trumps other values or ethical bases. The economic value lens is now the overarching narrative of our world. Something valuable is lost in making citizens become customers. To be identified merely as a customer is a narrow conception of being human.

The intrinsic value of the 'public sector model' itself thus suffered. Instead of upgrading the public service we tried to make it conform to a private sector model, management consultants, essentially accountants, were brought in. They imposed their own discipline - targets and new public management. The possibility of the public sector embracing their own kind of entrepreneurial spirit akin to that of the private sector, was lost.

Language matters. **Seeing people as citizens is different from seeing them as customers**. A citizen is more about 'me' and 'us' and how we form a society or joint identity and purpose. A customer is more about my wants, my needs, my desires. One is more relational and so about give and take or mutual interests. The other is more transactional thus 'do I get for what I pay for'? Interestingly what the public sector is losing, the deeper link to a citizen, private companies are trying to gain by creating product 'community' or brand or lifestyle associations.

Uneasy relationships

Bureaucrats have complex connections to navigate to make the most of possibilities

So bureaucrats ask: Should they drive change or just respond to it? Should they intervene or stand back? Should they lead policy thinking or wait to be advised by ministers, mayors, councillors or private sector entities? Should they let outside consultants do all the interesting work? Should they work in partnership with citizens or operate in secrecy?

This bigger context is exacerbated by an uneasy relationship between the bureaucracy and the elected government at all levels. There is a loss of trust in both directions. Short-term thinking can dominate. Internal power struggles have often led to arrangements to make it easier to 'hire and fire' employees, and sometimes this was the right thing to do, but it led to the increasing loss of influence of bureaucrats.

There are stories of bureaucratic incompetence that can't be blamed on those elected. These are the 'kafkaesque' experiences of people dealing with bureaucratic systems that seem to lack empathy or sense. These often operate in areas where people have the least power and are the most vulnerable, like social services, benefits or immigration.

The collaborative imperative

Organizations still tend to separate functions when many problems, like long term unemployment or mental health issues, require an integrated response across health, skills development or social care. Vertically siloed departments fight to grow their resources, not to collaborate and connect with others. Even when the weight of evidence favours connected thinking, collaboration is hard to achieve.

City development is still too frequently seen as a series of separate projects. Many rules are designed for single issues like health, safety, privacy, road guidelines, traffic flow or the environment. **Cities are complex and interconnected and so are issues**. Unemployment is not only about not having a job, social and mental health matters also come into play. A silo mentality over simplifies and separates that which needs to be connected. Interrelated issues like 'a vibrant environment' or 'a fairer city' require broader urban outcomes. They clearly need serious collaborative work across the sectors public, private and community.

Movements such as 'collaborative impact' are trying to overcome these separations. Here organizations agree on the deep changes they want to achieve and collaborate around them. In the small town of Medicine Hat in Canada[23], this approach was able to eliminate homelessness and their 'homeless first' strategy has even spread to larger places like Calgary.

The key skill for the 21st century for governments and bureaucracies is to partner with others across all parts of society. Only by doing this well will they have access to a wider set of intelligences, to create and tap into a wider pool of solutions, to generate more energy and resources. Short-term self-focused political gains need to give way to longer-term benefits. It remains a central task, difficult to achieve, and in a context of uncertainty. The tools of elected bodies, principally their policies and programmes, their bureaucracies and capital, have been shaped for eras of slow, steady and predictable change, not sudden often unpredictable shifts.

Multidisciplinary or Transdisciplinary

This implies that the city should be run more on interdisciplinary or transdisciplinary lines. In multidisciplinary approaches experts share information and knowledge, but are less likely to transform their own thinking. In the interdisciplinary world the aim and intent, say making a great place, is central. The only question then is how the expert discipline can help that goal.

Great, intelligent rules and incentives focus on what you want to achieve and empower you to get there. Too often a city has a vision and existing rules, often determined by a higher authority. Existing departmental structures add on strategies and actions to an existing sub-strata of rules, losing the intent of the vision.

The first step is to re-clarify a common intent, ambition for and picture of a place. The second is to ask 'do the regulations and laws help achieve the aims you want?' The incentives and regulations regime needs to adapt to get to where you want to go. The third step is whether staff at all levels are empowered and have incentives to connect the dots between the vision, the policy, the resources between the internal potential and the outside world. Too often they cannot or do not play this connector role.

The allure of the start-up

Levels of frustration are growing as bureaucracies have more highly educated employees than ever before. These employees are no longer content to be voiceless, to be infantilized or be treated as less intelligent or capable than they are. They are irritated that people think only the outsiders have clarity and clever ideas. They want to bring the sense of freedom and autonomy associated with start-up cultures to their day-to-day bureaucratic work. Public sector cultures which emphasise process, hierarchies or levels are rife with internal competition and are so increasingly less attractive to the most ambitious.

Bureaucrats know there are other ways to work out there. Their experiences in social networks and passion driven activities are more informal and adaptive. There they contribute within a community of equals. Technology helps create the exchange platforms that drive the necessary sharing. And the web 3.0, based on a world of sensorized objects, with its immersive, ever-present interactive capabilities and use of artificial intelligence, is set to change communication even more dramatically.

Younger bureaucrats take the new forms of communicating for granted

Bureaucracies need to help people feel this sense of freedom. The regularity, reliability and accountability of the bureaucratic form needs to meet the 'fleet of foot' of the digitally enabled world. They need to become empathetic environments that trigger a positive psychological response to bring the best out in people. Many new ways of running the public sector exist. Numerous examples are highlighted by the European Capital of Innovation – iCapital – award[24] which is described below.

Younger bureaucrats take the new forms of communicating for granted. They imagine services that return responsibility back to the individual. Critics and die-hards instantly label this as wanting to dismantle the welfare society. This is leading to a major upheaval of local governance. Yet the trend is clear. City hall has to support citizens' activities, with the community partially overtaking city government.

Old patterns of running organizations no longer work. They don't work for individual employees and they don't achieve the results they need. 'Bossing' people does not encourage them to give of their best. The focus increasingly is how to uncover, unlock and unleash potential. This calls for a different organizational ethos, different ideas of what leadership means and different behaviour patterns.

Equal relations with citizens

In the past restrictive attitudes were often etched into how codes were written. It led to an attitude that 'everything is forbidden unless it is allowed' rather than 'everything is allowed unless it is forbidden'. It's easier to say 'no' when regulations entwine at cross-purposes. Risk averse interpretation can neutralise good intentions. There is less the courage to say 'yes'.

Old patterns of running organizations no longer work

If systems intend to manage and control messages, they won't cope. **In the outside world citizens increasingly expect to be involved** in decisions that matter to them. They expect to have a say in creating services. They expect direct connections with decision makers. Bureaucrats and citizens see things changing rapidly. They do not want to be passive observers. Social media has changed the communications landscape. Everyone is 'constantly online'. They expect all forms of government to be transparent, responsive, accountable and good humoured.

Bureaucrats, who are also citizens, have the same expectations of the internal life of their bureaucracy. The trend is clear. Not everyone will want to be active or seen as shapers, makers and co-creators of their evolving environment. Many still shy away from participation and simply want things to work for them. But this should be their choice, not something imposed from above.

An era of shrinking resources

These movements are happening in an era of shrinking resources. Demands will continue to grow. Take health as an example. More provision can create more needs. Paradoxically, new resources may not meet demand, they stimulate it. Two approaches can address this. Get people to do things themselves or foster prevention. Technology is heading in this direction with gadgets that allow people to monitor their own health. But the system will need to change. Add to this an ageing population and the likely surge in demand for social services or mental care. Social health and mental care are connected and co-locating services, pooling funds and sharing costs across boundaries are obvious solutions. This is difficult to do, as cities like Helsinki have found out.

Blending the differing health and social service cultures is immensely difficult, but increasingly needs to happen. The health care culture is more immediate, emergency driven and faster whereas social care focuses more on the longer term in working with clients. Technology will help, such as automating processes, but will only be part of the answer. Most importantly, shrinking resources, pay restraints and low status and esteem can create a downward spiral which makes attracting and retaining good people difficult.

> The period for incremental adjustment is past...more dramatic change is required

Incremental adjustments will fail to cope. There is a need to think afresh, to experiment, to create new alliances and to combine ideas in new ways, to create new avenues for gaining revenue and resources. Governments, local and national, need to make an imaginative leap.

The emerging operating environment offers many more possibilities, but is impatient with or intolerant of nonsense rules. 'Nonsense rules' are the ways bureaucracies continue to regulate the working lives of their employees in trivial ways. It's the locked stationery cupboard in serious health and welfare organizations. It's the hazard signs advising not to eat photocopy toner or advising caution in walking around corridors. It's rules that prevent people exercising common sense, or taking normal risks.

The emerging environment is potentially more radical. It sees being trustful as key and connectedness as a driver of strategy making and as a means of adding value to projects and programmes.

Acting with foresight and agility

At the same time governments and bureaucracies are being called upon to think with foresight. To imagine how convoluted trends and countertrends may play out. This requires strategically agile, talented people.

The Dutch MVRDV project to create a liveable community in Taipei

Organizations are people and the quality of their thinking shapes the culture, rules and operating system. Any organization, public, private or community driven, should aim to be the best it can be to fulfil its intentions and ambitions. This involves harnessing the collective imagination, intelligence and capacities of those who work in them as well as able outsiders and partners – in short people and knowledge. This is their primary capital. Other assets: money, technology and physical things provide the back-up.

This is the context for the creative bureaucracy. The shifting landscape where committed and active bureaucrats at all levels of the organization work from their strengths. A capacity to innovate, exercise foresight and offer frank and fearless advice. Bureaucracies in a 21st century form – engaged, open, equal and imaginative. So how can the bureaucracy begin to shape this destiny?

... a 21st century form ... engaged, open, equal, and imaginative

THE 'LIVED EXPERIENCE': GOOD & BAD

The Critique

Conversations with bureaucrats in a dozen countries, perhaps 500 in all, at different levels give a flavour of their lived experience. We asked questions such as: How do you work at your best? What is blocking you to perform better? Describe the physical and cultural environment you would like and what needs to be done for you to be more fulfilled at work? They identified several reasons why bureaucracies are failing to inspire their people, reflecting many resentments.

Bureaucrats are committed to the tasks, they are essentially ready to be turned on and activated, excited by the possibilities and get glimpses of it. Given the freedom to talk, interviewees tended to focus on the negative. This is why in the section that immediately follows we summarize, by contrast, many examples of inventive bureaucracies and the people who work within them and how some bureaucrats have been able to make their mark. Seen positively the negative helpfully sets an agenda for the issues to be tackled. It also helps us to better appreciate the good examples of the public bureaucracy that are being achieved:

• **Bureaucrats are not publicly credited for their ideas** but their mistakes may be ruinous for them. The nature of government makes it hard for individuals to point to initiatives and to claim credit. In the world outside giving credit is more transparent.

• **Policy initiatives associated with former leaders**, governments or administrations, and which current employees helped create, are often abandoned whether or not they were effective.

• The **currency of internal power is influence** so there is an obsessive internal competition for influence or resources accompanied by an obsession with secrecy

• **A fear of getting things wrong** makes people reluctant to broach topics in case leaders react badly. Failure is insufficiently accepted. This constrains people as assumptions are made over what can be explored, discussed and done.

Bahrain, the desire for openness spills out everywhere

• **The 'not my job' syndrome** is exacerbated when people feel they have little control. People become inward looking and take a limited view of their jobs so failing to see the bigger picture or fail to develop the larger potential of projects because overly narrow thinking has become the norm.

• **'Reform fatigue'** and exhaustion with change programmes that paper over important issues, do not deal with bad managers or ineffective workers, and often parachute others in to senior roles.

• A **'culture of busyness'** leads people to equate being overscheduled with being important.

• There is always a pressure, but it is less a question of how you generate urgency, but **how you get rid of immediacy**.

... some problems feel intractable and a string of negatives need to be addressed

• **The power of connecting and partnering** with other departments, teams or organizations is rising in importance even though it is still insufficiently valued, supported or understood.

• **Procurement is thoughtlessly done** mostly and on a lowest cost basis - reducing the potential for innovation and potential spill-over benefits for local or small firms.

• **Poor performers are not dealt with** given the difficulty, even inability, to dismiss people or to allow for or manage conflict.

• **People get stuck**. The system should offer many opportunities yet formal employment processes make it hard for individuals to experiment with different roles and types of work. Some relish the idea of freelancing in government, working on projects, being in fluid team arrangements or working part time.

• Historically the senior management team would be **appointed from within the system**. People would work their way up. Now it is just as likely they will be appointed from outside or parachuted in to senior roles from the offices of ministers, senior consultants or private business. Those often intend to work only short term. So loyalty to an organization and deep knowledge of the bureaucracy can count against individual progress. Yet old stagers are also people who could, if conditions are right, challenge the system and question choices made.

• **Continuity of government was valued** – once. Today when a new government or council is elected they often replace the chief executive who then reconstitutes senior management teams.

The culture then becomes one of loyalty to the chief executive.

· **Consultants and academics are increasingly used** for policy advice and programme evaluation. This means that people interested in 'ideas' related work in government are more likely to have the opportunity to work on ideas from outside the administration.

· Managers and **senior staff had considerable leeway over their allocated budgets** in line with their formal delegated powers. Today there is intense scrutiny over even the smallest expenditures reducing the real authority associated with their senior roles.

· In many countries the **public service is dominated by people with a legal background**, who create a rigid culture that constrains possibilities.

· **A certain tolerance of mavericks** and eccentrics in the system was more evident in the past. These people may not have conformed but were often brilliant and valued for specialised knowledge or skills. They helped create a diversity of thought within the bureaucracy that made it relevant and imaginative. Yet cost cutting and more conformist attitudes do not let mavericks survive.

· **The bureaucracy is opaque** by its nature and seeks to avoid external scrutiny. This culture has persisted.

Reform fatigue was identified in the interviews and surveys as perhaps the major issue facing public administrators. Long-term employees may have experienced more than 10 major change programmes both in national or local government and within the internal organization. People become cynical and a 'we've been here before mentality' easily emerges.

'Shuffling the pack' and not addressing deeper issues leads to reform fatigue

Their frustration is not just that each new programme is sold as transformational, but it comes with implicit criticism of their performance. Crucially, it is also that most fail to deliver substantial change beyond a changing of the guard and new organizational titles.

Like the 'Gartner Hype Cycle'[25] people start with inflated expectations of what they can achieve. As they start to take action, others modify what they are allowed to do. They realise their goals won't be achieved. They sink into the 'trough of disillusionment' – some become depressed, others leave. Those that carry on achieve the 'plateau of productivity', accept the limitations and stay there.

Making it happen in Taipei: Jair Lin, a creative bureaucrat former head of the Urban Regeneration Office and Margaret Shiu, a great connector

Sir Cary Cooper co-author of 'High Engagement Work Culture: Balancing WE and ME' notes: '... the stresses we face in the workplace are generally no longer physical, they are other people... The line manager for all of us is absolutely fundamental to our wellbeing... the problem is that we recruited people... not on the basis of their social and interpersonal skills but on the long hours they worked, and their perceived effect on the bottom line, or whatever.'

The way we manage our employees has not kept pace with the changing nature of workplaces, growing competition and the changing attitudes of people at work. This mismatch is unsustainable.

The inspiration

Despite the obstacles felt by individuals within the bureaucracy, there are positive examples of bureaucratic change. Many of these are led by individuals who finally find themselves in a position to lead, influence and change systems. And, importantly, who have either the 'permission' to act or can operate sufficiently under the radar to lead changes.

In some cases a bureaucratic team has an enlightened idea that is replicable and spreads like wildfire, like participatory budgeting invented by Porto Alegre. We then forget it was very creative as it is assimilated. In other cases they exercise their influence within a domain – challenging rules and accepted practices. This is exemplified below by the story of Bill Bruce in Calgary. Others take on the system – introducing programmes that oblige people to work together in new ways, to tackle entrenched ways of thinking and to translate these approaches into on the ground action. This is exemplified by the work of Erma Ranieri in Adelaide.

Along the ways we can see new patterns to pushing and pulling change – inspired in some areas by impulses coming from outside government. Bureaucracies can't help but respond to the energy of entrepreneurialism; the disruptions offered by digital innovation; the passion and commitment of civic projects to do things for themselves and the ways the city can act as a platform for experimentation.

There are no other options. The grand challenges cities face will only be met if bureaucracies disrupt their own ways of working, give over control and work with people in business and the community as equal partners.

Systematic innovations are being incentivised by many new city based competitions. We describe one here – the European Capital of Innovation – where Charles has been the chair. Cities are inviting 'unconventional' thinking into the heart of administrations. Here we explore the role of Gabriella Gomez-Mont, an artist/film maker now city innovator in Laboratorio para de la Cuidad in Mexico City.

One way for cities to start is allowing temporary disruptions – through techniques such as 'tactical urbanism'. Here bureaucrats and citizens are invited to experiment, shock, inspire, engage in new ways. It builds the muscle for creativity- the consequences are rarely catastrophic.

While she is no longer working for the city, Helsinki invited and accepted the ideas of a then 24-year old to radically change the transport system with a focus on 'mobility as a service'. As the urgency of climate change becomes more apparent, and alternative transport options more available, transport is becoming a creative sphere where the city can act as a platform for ideas.

What is clear is that for cities to innovate they need the talents of creative bureaucrats prepared to experiment (and risk their careers) in pursuit of systematic changes.

Cities are inviting 'unconventional' thinking into their administrations

The Emscher Park IBA

The challenge for cities is that imaginative bureaucrats must deal with existing conditions to implement their vision. Emscher Park an emblematic project in the Ruhr developed in the 1990s is worth highlighting as a pioneer. It reimagined the potential of the vast industrial region. It was a project of the Internationale Bauaustellung (IBA). The IBA is a German government initiative that identifies areas in need of transformation and provides these with long term resources to make change. The Emscher Park was led by Karl Ganser a former senior civil servant who was able to iterate around what he called 'incrementalism with perspective'. Driven by a strong ethos to combine cultural renewal projects, social change and environmentalism he could orchestrate and combine isolated decentralised projects so that they could become part of a coherent whole. But his success relied on the IBA being an arm's length organization — 'part of, but not part of the public structures' and so able to 'decrust the old system' as 'institutional immobilism' was seen as the block.

The IBA was not an agency nor a plan in the traditional sense. It had a perspective on development and played an advisory role with local projects. It had no money, nor competences in law. It had no direct power, only leverage given by the ministry as it accredited projects that more or less guaranteed resourcing from regional government or the European Union. It also helped bundle resources and acted as a branding device and quality benchmark for projects with its logo. This gave it prestige and status.

It kept out of local politics that some later criticized as when the 10 year project finished they felt it was not deeply enough embedded. By this means an attempt was made to take the IBA above and out of politics. Ganser and his team could be creative bureaucrats without needing to pull along a bureaucracy or many of its political leaders. This enabled his team to experiment, such as with housing formats and the deadline for the overall project created momentum. The IBA stated there are no ideals but only project models and saw itself as a dispersed experimentation zone based on a series of learning projects. The IBA's core mechanism was to mobilize expectations through the propaganda of a the good creative example.[26]

Can we change the rules? Visitor looking at Alex Buldakow's work at Frieze, London

Participatory budgeting[27]

We forget how some bureaucratic innovations with strong impact have become mainstream yet were once very creative. One such is participatory budgeting. This refers to how citizens and local officials come together to work out a list of priorities to direct public funding, which the larger community then votes on. Porto Alegre in Brazil invented the concept in 1989 (as it did the World Social Forum in 2001) as it wanted to encourage popular participation in governance and redirect resources to the poor. Since then there have been 1500 examples across the five continents and it is promoted by the European Union, the World Bank and the United Nations even though it is not yet common practice. The first African examples came out of the Yaounde meeting in 2003; various European ones emerged in Italy and Spain in the early to mid-2000s; in North America first in Toronto in 2001 and in the States in Chicago in 2009 with others following in China and elsewhere in Asia at the same time.

... some innovations can catch on like wild fire

The advantage is that individuals and communities feel empowered, listened to and engaged. They share the understanding of the difficulties of making choices between equally important projects. **The shared responsibility results in greater trust** as they take decisions together and have an idea of the priorities, choices and consequences. When cities are faced with cuts this is important.

Examples of projects voted through are extensive and very diverse. Paris, one of the biggest schemes, has allocated more than €20 million per annum until 2020 (5% of the city budget). Top voted initiatives include walled gardens, urban renewal projects, co-working for students and young entrepreneurs, improved waste sorting, school gardens, composting and recycling initiatives, and more. Seoul now puts $50 million annually into projects voted on by members of the Participatory Budget Council comprising people from school children to elders. In 2013, the top-voted projects included expanding the facilities for people with disabilities at a local sports centre; creating community projects to stop bullying and school violence; installing gas safety valves in homes of the low-income retirees living alone; and creating a community restaurant that makes dishes with bean sprouts grown in senior centres. Toronto's scheme allocates funds, ranging from $5 million to $9 million, to community housing residents who have voted on community gardens, safety upgrades, entryway improvements and building playgrounds.

Competitions trigger ambition: The European Capital of Innovation[28]

How do you begin to change government and city systems? One way is through competitions. The competition for the European Capital of Innovation is helping to shape city innovation systems across sectors, ways of thinking, design and imagination. Impulses for change can come from multiple directions. It's essential to solve problems with citizens in imaginative ways. Cities engage with SMEs and help them test and experiment in real settings, and by so doing build a reputation needed for commercial success. Our direct involvement has given us insight into how the public administrations of European cities are exercising imagination and foresight.

The criteria used in 2017 are:

• Experimenting with innovative concepts, processes, tools, and governance models as prototypes.

• Engaging citizens in the innovation process and ensuring the uptake of their ideas.

• Expanding the city's attractiveness to become a role model for other cities.

• Empowering the local ecosystem through the implementation of innovative practices.

This is aligned to the idea of 'civic creativity'. City systems, people, place, the private and public realms are interconnected. **Together they can create interactive, innovative ecosystems**. Over 120 cities have participated in the competition to date, including the very large, such as Paris, Berlin, Barcelona and Amsterdam; mid-sized cities such as Torino, Grenoble to smaller cities such as Groningen or Modena.

We describe some of the ideas developed by the winners and runners up in the competition. They demonstrate that cities can be laboratories for experimentation so unleashing new types of energy and engagement. Their experiences also help us understand the impediments to change.

Two core issues emerged from all finalists. First, the biggest obstacle to change was their own municipal institutions and the need to overcome the silo mentality. Second, they stressed the difficulties in achieving real collaboration, connectivity between the various players in order to benefit from networking[29].

It takes more than just a good idea to win, intent was not enough. Cities have to show concrete results of their projects as well as a track record of innovation. Most importantly, they needed to demonstrate an interconnected innovation eco-system approach. This means involving citizens, universities, the public and private sectors. A number of themes emerge:

… the biggest obstacles were their municipal institutions

• Open data applications – such as crowd-sourcing ideas find and fund solutions to urban problems ranging from crime prevention, to energy saving, to dealing with traffic problems. This is now becoming mainstream.

• Addressing the energy transition using incentives and regulations in imaginative ways. The goal being to change faster than mandated reduction targets.

• Reconceptualising complete systems – for example citizens aided by technology to manage and maintain their own health. Health is personalised, the user is in control of when and how they access systems.

• 'Living labs' that act as models for changing city systems. These typically combine incentives to develop the creative economy, eco-city thinking, new forms of mobility and co-creation.

• Inviting SMEs to use the city as a test bed for innovations to help solve urban problems. Companies can then prototype inventions and use the city brand as a marketing tool.

Barcelona won the first award in 2014 for introducing 'new technologies to bring the city closer to citizens' emphasizing 'technology for people'. For instance, teaching the elderly to use smart phones to communicate with their doctors. An unintended consequence was many were able to communicate with their grandchildren in new ways. Most applications were co-created with citizen groups and business. Crucially the city had a focus on sharing results.

Amsterdam argued that the fight against floods since the 16th century has forced the city to collaborate, but its 21st century version embraces openness, pragmatism and adaptiveness. It won the second award in 2016 for its holistic vision connecting four areas of urban life: governance, economics, social inclusion, and quality of life. Citizens use technology to have new types of conversations and solve problems from fixing a broken paving stone to a conscious orchestration of 'serendipity' through virtual and real 'meeting places'. The Pakhuis de Zwijger is an independent platform and place for inspiration and joint problem solving. The Amsterdam Institute for Advanced Metropolitan Solutions is a well-funded living lab to develop and test complex metropolitan solutions – involving the Amsterdam citizens as testers, users and co-creators.

Paris, a runner up, opened municipally-owned property (streets, gardens, buildings, basements, schools) to experimental innovative solutions. Innovations were invited through calls for proposals, around a theme, from all types of businesses. The premise is that the sum of collective intelligence outside an organization is always greater than the knowledge within. By opening out and exchanging information, this collective intelligence can be channelled.

Groningen, a runner up, created tools and processes to develop a user-centred smart energy ecosystem. Called the 'smart energy citizen' the aim is to shift the power in energy markets from large energy providers to groups of citizens. It used imaginative communications to foster behaviour change such as heat maps for the whole city to show where and how much energy is used.

Espoo, part of the Helsinki city region and a finalist, established a strategic partnership uniting science, business and artistic creativity. The location of Nokia and major game companies Rovio (Angry Birds) and Supercell (The Clash of Clans) unites these elements. Aalto University is a unique merger of an art and design university with one focusing on science and technology and a business school.

Torino faces a dramatic transition from an industrial city to a centre of innovation and culture. It was essentially a Fiat city with nearly 100,000 workers 40 years ago. Now there are only a few thousand. It is rethinking connections – developing trust through horizontal partnerships, trying to be lean (as they say: 'no rigidity in the procedures, to support the fluid and risk taking process of innovation'). They say in the context of Italy this is creative.

Rules & social capital

Rules can build social capital as Bill Bruce Calgary's director of By-Laws known as 'By-law Bill' showed. Internationally known he retired in 2012 and he was a masterful creative bureaucrat whom Charles met in 2006. He is an inspiration and he worked with the city for 32 years and his vision was to work on solutions rather than heavy-handed enforcement, since as he notes: 'If I enforced every law, provincial and city, I'd have every citizen in court for something, including you and me.' His ethos is embodied in the community standards bylaw he helped to write.[30] [31]

One example was ensuring safety on the 650 kilometres of shared-use pathways jointly used by walkers, cyclists, skateboarders and roller-bladers, runners and dog walkers. One rule is that all bicycles have to have a bell to alert other users. The penalty for failing to have one in 2006 was a $87.00 fine. Failing to pay had further consequences. Historically, officers would patrol the pathway and stop cyclists without a bell and fine them. These interactions were unpleasant and stressful for both the officer and cyclist. After the confrontation the cyclist would ride away angry with their $87.00 ticket but still with no bell on the bike – no compliance. Administering the fine cost the taxpayer $100 and more if the cyclist ended up in court. The simple solution was to revisit the original goal of compliance and to review options to achieve it. The city was able to buy 100 bells wholesale at $1.00 per bell and 12 screwdrivers for each of the rangers.

Officers were given bells and a screwdriver with the instruction to continue to enforce the regulation but to do it differently. During the dialogue with 'offenders', the officer covers the reasons why the bell is needed and the penalty for noncompliance. He then says they are lucky as he has a bell and a screw driver and if the cyclist is willing to install it now, the officer will not give them a ticket. During the installation time, the officer takes advantage to continue the positive dialogue and educate the cyclist on other safety related regulations. At the end of this five- to ten-minute encounter, the cyclist rides away in compliance, educated and in a positive mood as they have been given a gift. The officer returns to duty after a constructive, unstressful encounter. The prime goal of compliance is achieved. To date, no one has declined to accept the bell and take the ticket option. This approach is far cheaper. Crucially with financial capital, the more you use it the less you have; with social capital the more you use it the more it achieves.

Innovating against the grain

The Creative Administration in Bizkaia project explored how the innovation department of the Bilbao region was itself innovative. Undertaken by Charles it was commissioned by the Bizkaia Economic Promotion Department (BEPD) and Bilbao Metropoli 30 in 2010. It was a courageous move to allow an outsider in. Not many cities are willing to undertake such a self-reflection itself a creative act. The department had 150 people including its related delivery agencies and people were interviewed from the top, level one, to level seven the secretarial staff.

National laws can limit the scope to act so making cities seem inflexible

The Bilbao region is known for its innovative and emblematic urban regeneration initiatives and talent attraction strategies. At the same time its bureaucratic system is governed and hampered by the national Spanish 'administration law.' This limits the scope to act. The lesson we highlight here is how a bigger system constrains potential. This law reflected its time and context and handcuffs organizational development in tune with today's situation. It enforces rigidity in terms of procedures, employment flexibility and recruitment practices. For instance, it seemed impossible to substitute an existing underperforming worker with a very good, young unemployed person.

This is significant because BEPD's principle role is to foster innovation and company development and to attend to the strategic orchestration of the creativity agenda itself, which implies displaying some of the creativity it is seeking to foster. But internally BEPD had to operate in relatively traditional ways even though it knows that leaders, managers and staff need to model the intent of the organization by being switched on, flexible, experimental. This they could not be then.

The way entrance exams for public service work **means a legal mind and knowledge is privileged**. Consequently proportionately more lawyers are in the service than one would expect. Additionally the exam system and the public administration law determine the status and position of employees entering public service. This can hamper developing the talent pool by creating a glass ceiling for some who in other circumstances would be promoted. Additionally the system tends to dissuade precisely those it needs to to attract such as younger people more adept with communication tools.

The dominant mindset that shapes how public organizations in the Spanish context (and in Germany and Italy too) operate is **the 'culture of the lawyer'**. This thinking might not help achieve innovation objectives, or foster emotional intelligence, where staff may require a different skillset. The 'culture of the lawyer' is so strong that departments, such as tax, public works or public administration have stronger status in comparison to economic development. BEPD procedures then reflected the requirements of the public administration 'law' rather than what might be right for BEPD's needs.

This prescribes how things are to be done in far too much detail, such as the level of checking to write out a cheque. Called the 'endless procedure' it can apparently take up to a dozen checks to expedite some cheques. These laws require people to make extra efforts to work around constraints often wasting energy. The legal culture makes it difficult to test these laws or to review them. In that context the central question is what aspects of BEPD's organizational culture are system driven and which are to do with people and their operating styles. It is both, they are inextricably interwoven.

The setting described shapes the organizational culture. Many members of staff had a long organizational history and they carried an institutional memory stretching back 25 years. Over this period the leadership changed a number of times. In the periods when staff felt involved and included, interviewees said, it increased their motivation, work rate and effectiveness. They felt listened to and valued as staff satisfaction surveys were acted upon.

... long-winded, complex procedures can drain the spirit

An informal poll suggested that in the good periods, people worked to 80%+ of their potential capacity and in less good periods down to 60% or even less. Here they stressed they put energy into their private life and as someone at level six noted 'they don't pay me to think'. It encapsulates how important an inclusive work environment is.

Mobility as a service

In 2014, the city of Helsinki announced that it planned to move to a system now known as 'mobility as a service'. Its effect would be to provide a seamless public transport service based around peoples' individual travel preferences rather than the needs of the system. **This apparently simple switch is a paradigm shift in public transport thinking**. The aim is to combine all modes of transport from public and private operators including public buses, trams and trains and our cars and bikes.

It changes the perception of transportation away from separate, individual providers to a mobility-centric system. It works by leveraging the digital revolution and peoples' mobiles to pay for kilometre-based mobility packages, rather than multiple tickets for individual rides as well as acting as a virtual payment system.

... services like transport or social services can be completely rethought

It combines regular timetabled services with the ability to summon on-demand rides from a variety of public and private services. This way bus routes and the activities of private operators become dynamic, because the consistent platform enables multiple operators to offer a seamless service through one ticketing system. By getting people seamlessly from one point to another across transportation modes it would, in effect, eliminate the need for private car ownership. The aim is to get to a point where owning your own vehicle is unnecessary. Helsinki believes the system could be in place by 2025.

Even now, in 2017, this is a radical proposal. What made it even more so was that the city commissioned the work from transport engineering student, Sonja Heikkila, then aged 24, who developed the thinking through her Master's thesis.

The then head of the city's transport section supported the idea, planned to invest in testing it, and promoted Heikkila as the author. She has received international attention for her work. **She imagined boldly what transport could be:** 'A car is no longer a status symbol for young people' she said. On the other hand young people are more adamant in demanding simple, flexible and inexpensive transportation. She pointed to the telecommunications industry as an example of how services could be provided in a way that differs from the current model.

This example is interesting for a number of reasons. It signals that Helsinki is prepared to think afresh. This may have catalytic spillover effects, such as assessing the effect of driverless vehicles. It gets people to think how this might signal a radical transformation for cities. It gets people to think about the impact of robots on employment or on systems like health care where a loss of 40% of jobs is predicted by 2025. 'How' concentrates the mind and makes the local and national government think what it should be doing now.

The city commissioned a young woman to develop the idea and allowed her to be its public face. In many places such work would have been commissioned from expensive consulting companies. It would have been branded with the name of the company. Announcements would have been made by senior leaders. Any public servants involved in the project would have remained anonymous.

Adelaide 90 day projects

After more than 25 years in the public sector Erma Ranieri was ready for big challenges when she was appointed to head up the Public Sector Renewal programme in South Australia. **She wanted to infuse positive energy into the system** whilst taking on sector- wide problems. She felt that public servants could solve big problems if given the chance and the right structures, to do so. The response was the '90-Day Project'. These projects share a number of important elements.

• Each 90-Day project is framed around a specific challenge. Each is sponsored by the State Premier and has Cabinet priority – signalling its importance. Projects are selected with care, they matter.

• The 90-day timeframe provides a sense of urgency and a constraint. Projects can't drag on – they have to come to a conclusion.

• Public servants volunteer to participate. They are expected to think creativity, to take risks and to consult with users. It's energising to be a part of a 90-day project.

• They combine people in new ways – across normal agency boundaries. People get to see the challenge from new perspectives, to understand the system context. More importantly they also see the user or citizen context.

• A key ambition is for the public sector to act as 'one government'. All the projects involve collaboration across agency boundaries. They also engage the users of services - citizens.

bureaucratic inventiveness Is growing across the world

Ultimately the aim is to transform the system itself, in positive ways that build the confidence of bureaucrats, political leaders and citizens.

Projects have ranged from health, industry development, environmental improvements, police operations, transport development and beyond.

An initial 90 Day project brought community service organizations together with government agencies to understand how to align efforts and improve impact. This has led to new cross agency working arrangements and to providers working together to achieve 'collective impact'.

Another project focused on creating a 'State of Well Being'[32] based on the work of renowned positive psychologist, Martin Seligman. This has led to an ongoing programme for community resilience and well-being. There have also been projects to improve experiences of the health system for patients. Another took on how to make the private rental market fairer in South Australia. A further project quickly brought the fragmented music industry together to better support artists so that they could create a more vibrant music scene. It stimulates connections and innovation – between digital and music and the potential benefits of music in other sectors. Erma is now the Commissioner for Public Employment, still with responsibility for public sector renewal and 90 day Projects.

Living labs & urban laboratories

The Living Lab Movement is an important development and there are several hundred across the world. Here users shape innovation in their own real-life environments, whereas in traditional innovation networks the insights of users are captured and interpreted by experts. **Many initiatives focus on social innovations** and look at issues from the street upwards. Belgium, the Netherlands and Finland are leaders in Europe in using Labs to harvest creativity. Flanders and Brussels have co-created funds to develop public innovations adapted to projects coming out of Labs. This has meant taking away or changing rules.[33]

Mexico City's Laboratorio para la Ciudad[34] founded in 2013 and launched by Gabriella Gomez Mont is exceptional. It is an experimental think and do tank for the city government. Politically courageous, it employs a multidisciplinary team of 22 people, including political scientists, artists, planners, anthropologists, photographers and lawyers. Their views are fresh and they engage under-represented communities across the city and make calls to gather ideas or to solve problems for example by developing apps. One crowd sourced a route map for the myriad official and semi-official minibuses that crisscross the city. They also acted as a negotiator to solve the escalating Uber versus traditional taxi conflict that resulted in an agreed new levy to help the transport system. A strong focus has been on creating public play areas for the nearly five million children in the city, whose needs are largely neglected. In addition their community visioning work is helping the city administration reorient its services. Naturally working with and against the bureaucracy in imaginative ways is challenging.

Woensel West & Trudo

A similar inspirational semi-public initiative is Woensel West. It is an extension of the Strijp-S renewal project in the old Phillips areas in Eindhoven into housing, mixed use and incubation centres by a social housing company Trudo. The neighbourhood had received special 'urban renewal status' whose goal was to end 'deprivation' with extra budgets to renovate houses, improve public space and to organize social activities. It failed partly because of the decline of Philips, secondly many people leaving psychiatric institutions were housed in the district.

Trudo was convinced traditional policies would not work. They needed a dramatic game changer as the local school had to be closed down because of heroin trading. In spite of threats it started with security and, in collaboration with the police, they dealt with drugs and prostitution. The clever solution was a scheme whereby students give their time freely to help the underprivileged in exchange for cheap rents. This immensely successful project has transformed a failing school to one of the best in the province.

Challenge as opportunity

Bergen hosted the Road Cycling World Championships one of cycling greatest events over nine days in September 2017 and wanted to engage citizens and create a spectacular. It attracted several hundred thousand spectators. It was broadcast to 300 million viewers world-wide.

How then to maintain vital functions like safety, health care, electricity and to ensure infrastructure with large areas of the city isolated. Add the higher risks and need for security. The biggest problem was coordinating the 31 agencies in charge of critical services ranging from private companies to public agencies belonging to the city, region or state.

Their answer was the Interagency Cooperation Center, not an operation center but a cluster of intertwined agencies vital to the city's everyday functioning and crisis management. The differing organizations kept their respective chains-of-command.

The ICC's main tasks are: real-time monitoring, gathering and sharing information, ensuring good communication and coordination, mapping resources, clarifying and recommending common guidelines. The results were astonishing. **Interagency cooperation resolved problems in minutes**, that normally would take hours or days. Crucially incidents were solved before they became large and expensive. Resolving incidents when still small meant there was no need to involve higher level decision-makers.

A similar collaborative process happened when Helsinki won the Eurovision contest in 2006 with the heavy metal band Lordi. As host for the 2007 competition with widespread celebrations in the city the administration developed a joint action committee rather like Bergen and it was equally effective. These are good examples of crises, yet a negative one can also at times have a positive outcome.

THE BUREAUCRATIC DYNAMIC

Light is breaking out in many areas. But risk aversion trumps imaginative thinking – mostly. Governments and public administrations are falling behind as they retreat to the tried and true.

Crisis, of course, is not always joyful. When disasters happen it often triggers a rethinking of procedures that then become mainstream. Many operate as if the future will be much like the past. That change will be steady and incremental. They have not yet viscerally imagined how the systems or the cultures of today will suit a future where a predict and provide model won't work.

Most are not capable of radical rethinking and farsighted strategy. Many'... respond to the most disruptive changes by accelerating the activities that succeeded in the past'.[35] This idea of 'active inertia' by academic, Donald Sull, describes this state of doing more of the same because it worked in the past. Kodak is one of the best known examples from the private sector.

The alternative is to get more comfortable with uncertainty. To anticipate and **prepare for opportunities and threats which cannot be 'controlled'**. But the idea that you have the power and authority to direct the world is hard to let go of. This is understandable. Citizens want answers and precise plans. So bureaucracies and political leaders act as though they can and will deliver solutions. And they turn to things they did in the past, rather than embrace the opportunities of the future.

'The very DNA of bureaucratic organization is resistant to innovation' suggests Christian Bason formerly of Mindlab, a Danish organization promoting bureaucratic innovation. Bureaucracies work at several levels and collectively constrain the possibilities to be innovative. Eight are highlighted:

A default position to control rather than engage. Those at lower levels can have little autonomy to interpret or tailor rules and procedures to individual circumstances. This, in turn, detaches the administration from the people it serves as well as with others in the bureaucracy. It can make the organization seem faceless.

Bahrain: Light is breaking out in the bureaucracy

Krakow: Great forces pull officials in different directions

Being purposefully impersonal: Individual bureaucrats are rarely acknowledged in public. They can't take credit for authoring policies, articles, books or innovations. Invisibility can make the organization an easier target. Once you see the person behind the work attitudes can shift and soften. More context can help people understand the difficult choices an administrator needs to make. Bureaucrats need credit and acknowledgement too.

Segregating functions: Our world is increasingly connected but our work programmes are not. A great organization integrates specialist, generalist and cross-cutting knowledge. It values diverse thinking. It needs those who can grasp the essence of issues, those who think in abstract terms and those who have the emotional intelligence to bring the best out in people. This offers the greatest potential for creating public value and even reducing costs.

An obvious illustration is health. People are healthier in walkable and compact cities. Urban sprawl is associated with obesity, pollution and sedentary behaviour, resulting in massive drains on public expenditure. Despite the connections being well known, it is still difficult to create transport or urban programmes that prioritise citizen health.

Budgets rigidly controlled and fully allocated: It can be hard to reallocate funding from one portfolio area to another. Increased scrutiny of expenditure makes organizations and bureaucrats fearful. Control of a budget represents power. The incentive is to accrue and control – not share or collaborate, adjust thinking or recognise a priority elsewhere.

The system is also to blame. Enlightened administrators may want to leverage resources by combining with others. Yet once allocated, say to a transport project, it is nigh impossible to shift that to urban design or an activity programme. Or the rules favour expensive capital projects when modest revenue projects are needed.

Ideas come from senior levels: Major ideas or policy generation happens in the power play between politicians and senior staff. This misses the potential of learning from the many people in middle and lower levels or from citizens, the community or business. They may understand better the nuances of how a project or programme could work.

Good ideas can come from many directions

Ideas need many champions to go forward, but only one person to stop them. The impulse is to critique, not to imagine or to take a risk. Ideas ahead of their time, that require collaboration across agencies, or which are not already supported higher up the line are easier to dismiss.

Intrapreneurship is a version of ideas generation – the act of behaving like an entrepreneur while working within a large organization. It is crucial if bureaucracies want to stay alive. Most famously Art Frey, a mid-level employee at 3M invented the Post-It note as he recognised that an adhesive invented internally that wasn't completely rock solid could solve his everyday problem of bookmarks falling out of his reading book. Paul Buchheit at Google created the initial template for Gmail. DreamWorks offer their employees free classes, from script development to pitching, and encourage them to present the best in front of the company's executive team. Google's most famous management philosophy '20% time' is emblematic even though only about 10% of Googlers are free enough to use it.

Secrecy: In some public bureaucracies, including universities, individuals and teams are reluctant to share their ideas. Status, credibility and promotion can depend on - or resources can flow toward — those recognised as the creator of an idea that gains favour. Getting things wrong can have dire consequences.

Consultants are widely used because they bring ideas to an organization, are not protective of them and they may take risks. They can often 'cut through' in ways those inside cannot. Inside, people that have ideas stand out and become a target - both good and bad.

Many **bureaucracies have a default position that everything is confidential**. It may have plausible rationale but it can go too far. More and more things become guarded information, diaries and appointments, even internal physical access. This fosters paranoia. Local authorities are more transparent. Their open meetings make it necessary. Some bureaucracies are embracing radical transparency. Helsinki citizens can explore the documents decision makers are using through the Ahjo case management system.[36]

Public procurement strategies shape local markets. They can help local companies and start-ups gain access to global markets. They can encourage innovation. But they often favour large, established global firms and tried and true methods. In the European Union public procurement accounts for 14% of GDP and the European Commission notes: 'The potential of public procurement to foster innovation remains vastly untapped."[37] This is not only to encourage innovations within firms, but also to trigger innovations within the public sector itself. Crucially, since the sector structures the regulatory context in which innovation takes place, by being innovative itself, it will understand innovation better.[38]

One reason for being conservative and focused on processes in procurement is to safeguard against nepotism and corruption. Another is to avoid criticism. There is also a belief that specifying all the requirements in detail up front avoids risks. But this also limits innovation. The public sector usually knows less about what the market and citizen's groups could in principle, offer. New methods are being trialled by organizations such as Citymart.[40] This group seeks to transform the way cities solve problems. Their approach called **'problem-based procurement' tries to connect cities to new ideas** through open challenges to entrepreneurs and citizens. It does this by packaging problems or tasks, the terms of procurement, qualifications and evaluation criteria into a user-friendly, easy-to-understand open challenge. This changes the method cities use for buying goods and services. It uses the existing structure but brings in new actors so opening up possibilities for not yet thought of solutions.

The trust issue: One of the major challenges for governments and their administrations is that the public lacks confidence in them. An OECD report of 2017[41] suggests only 40% trust their national government. Trust declined strongly since 2007 unsurprisingly in Greece, Portugal and Spain where trust levels are around 20%, but has risen in Germany to 60%.

Trust in local and regional government is far higher mostly because they are closer to the citizen. A decline since 2008 is perceptible but smaller. Taking Europe as a whole in Northern Europe trust is 66% a decline of 5%; in Central and Eastern Europe 38% down by 3%, in Western Europe 56% down by 1% and Southern Europe down by 12% at 28%.[42]

A 2015 survey of the US Federal Government found that only 20% of the public believed that federal programmes were well run. 59% thought the federal government was in need of major reform. Only 19% trusted the government 'always or most of the time'. Less than 50% ranked the government for handling 'wicked issues' like getting people out of poverty. With the Trump administration will these results remain the same?

Public bureaucracies face pressures internally, externally and through perceptions of what they can achieve. Faced with such circumstances they respond by announcing a restructure, effectively shuffling the pack, instead of asking how the deeper nuances of the organization can shift. This distracts energy and consumes resources needed to respond to the change.

Indeed there are many things that bureaucracies could and should be doing to build their capabilities and creative potential. And in principle they know what this is. Thoughtful and progressive organizations across public and private worlds know they need to engage, connect, experiment and grow their comfort around ideas and innovation. They need a **radical transformation in culture towards openness**. Bureaucracies need to build the energy and warmth of their organizations that make them places safe for ideas and for people. Models of command and control do not bring out the best in people. Some find talk of organizational warmth woolly and vague, but it may be the hidden ingredient that makes places work.

It's not hard to find good examples or to access the latest thinking from across the world, to learn from their practices or to test their impact. So why is it rarely done well by bureaucracies?

Progressive organizations are engaging their constituencies far more strongly

SELF-REALIZATION & WORK

Dramatic evidence suggests that creativity is the most sought after attribute in successful organizations – private or public.

Since 2004 IBM has been undertaking biennial Global CEO studies with the largest known sample of one-on-one CEO interviews, with over 1,500 corporate heads and public sector leaders across 60 nations and 33 industries. They include related surveys with 3600 students from over 100 major universities around the world whom they consider to be future leaders. CEOs were polled on what drives them in managing their organizations today. Since the studies started in 2004 'creativity' and 'adaptiveness', 'partnering across boundaries' have been consistent themes as part of IBM's central question 'are you ready to face the unfolding world?' The 2010 study concludes that creativity (60%) is the most important leadership quality for success, outweighing even integrity (52%) and global thinking (38%). Another IBM study, specifically of public sector leaders, 'Capitalizing on Complexity' states:

'The world's private and public sector leaders **identify 'creativity' as the single most important leadership competency** for enterprises seeking a path through complexity.'

The most important characteristic for CEOs, public and private sector leaders agreed, is to embody creative leadership. Creative leaders are comfortable with ambiguity and experimentation and use it to capitalise on complexity.[43]

Public sector leaders agreed they needed to encourage openness, and experimentation within their organizations. They rated the need to get closer to citizens, their customers and co-create services as one of the top priorities. They rated accessing insight and intelligence even higher than private sector CEOs. They felt, too, that they were a long way behind industry 'standouts'.

The studies found that public sector leaders didn't feel well prepared to handle complexity and that this gap in capability was greater than that faced by CEOs in the private sector. In fact it was the largest IBM had measured in the eight years they had been conducting this research.

*ndon: Re-
*aking urban
*frastructure
*volves a
*ultitude of
*zards and
oices

In addition they stress that: 'the speed at which CEOs across the spectrum are opening the doors to enable collaboration is extraordinary'. A growing number of private sector CEOs, so IBM has found, believe customer influence should not be merely confined to traditional activities, such as developing new products or services. Instead, increasingly **CEOs believe they should stand ready to relinquish absolute control** of what is typically considered their domain, namely developing business strategy. They see greater organizational openness ahead, but like public administrations, private entities are worried how they can avoid chaos and still deliver results as rules are refined and collaboration explodes. One of these is the civic explosion expressed, for instance, by the Impact Hub network and movement with over 100 centres across five continents and more than 15,000 members. These offers space, a community, and a global platform to support social innovators. They are a combination of 'an innovation lab, a business incubator and a social enterprise community centre offering a unique ecosystem of resources, inspiration, and collaboration opportunities to grow positive impact'. Public bureaucracies cannot neglect them.

... public and private sectors need to respond to the rise of civic activism

Most organizations find the concept of 'creativity' a difficult one. It, therefore, begs the question- how will the leaders of the future develop their own creativity? It has to start with creativity being valued generally across organizations.

The former head of innovation at Nissan, Jerry Hirshberg , who wrote The Creative Imperative calls the bureaucracy the 'perfect idea killing machine':

'No-one... deliberately sets out to stifle creative thought. Yet, a traditional bureaucratic structure, with its needs for predictability, linear logic, conformance to accepted norms, and the dictates of the most recent 'long range' vision statement, is a nearly perfect idea killing machine.'

There are exceptions and several private companies are leading the way. Take Britain's John Lewis/Waitrose, a major department store and retailer. As a cooperative every employee is a co-owner and shares in its success. So commitment and loyalty is a given. Employees and managers alike understand that self-determination is key. That means setting your own path and being accountable for success and failure. Nurturing this individuality means abandoning some orderliness and elements of structure. Letting people be themselves, interestingly, seems to enable people to be a part of something bigger than themselves or becoming and being their better selves.

Waitrose sees its edge in fostering sparks of creativity by supporting people's personal interests. If you want to learn piano, for instance, Waitrose will pay half the cost. A thought experiment: Is there a way of co-owning the bureaucracy?

Creativity stands in opposition to traditional bureaucratic values – a formal hierarchy, defined classifications and authority structures, micro management tendencies and a surfeit of rules.

It is not surprising that those rising through the system often do not bring the perspectives and dynamism needed for senior ranks, having not been able to explore and experiment previously. So talented outsiders, with little invested in the way things are now, are brought in. They bring fresh perspectives, often on high salaries. But their external ideas can fail to embed or be sustained over time. This can create internal tensions.

Bureaucracies reduce talent by training the brightest to conform

So here is a dilemma. The bureaucracy systematically reduces the quality of its talent. I**t recruits many of the brightest. It trains them to conform**. It creates rule followers. The more independently minded leave. The public administration is without the talent it needs to lead for the future. All individuals have an inner impulse to express themselves, to create and to be seen. We all have to find ways to express this energy.

This is why the idea of 'the side project' in peoples' lives has become fashionable. There is an important distinction between a 'side project' and a hobby. The latter implies relaxing into and giving time to your personal interests. The former is about giving the energy and commitment you would ideally want to express at work to an outside cause be it helping the homeless, being part of a start-up, or a local area management committee. Yet our work in Bilbao and Adelaide and that of Adobe, IBM and Gallup demonstrates that **bureaucrats remain hopeful they will be engaged, inspired**, uplifted and challenged.

Adobe's[44] global benchmark study, of 5000 adults across the world, explored attitudes and beliefs about creativity at work, school and home. Over 80% agreed that 'unlocking creative

potential is key to economic and societal growth'. Yet 'less than half describe themselves as creative'. Only one in four people feel they are living up to their creative potential at work, especially given the increasing pressure to be productive rather than creative at work.

People spend only 25% of their time at work thinking ahead, questioning the tried and tested, being imaginative, exploring new ground, creating or solving problems or searching for potentials. Whereas they spend 31% of their time being creative at home. 61% believe that the ability to be imaginative and creative defines a person. 77% believe it enables them to make a difference in their lives and 62% to the lives of others. 69% say they are willing to share the fruits of their creativity. Over 80% believe we all have the potential to create and that creativity begins with an environment where people can explore and express ideas. Time, money and self-doubt are seen as the biggest challenges to being able to create.

A US survey of government workers found that while 86% felt they could make a difference and 87% were proud to work in government, only 31% strongly felt that they were valued and 58% felt fully engaged with their job.[45]

A survey of Irish civil servants found that while 92% were confident in their ability to do their job only 42% felt the job utilised their full abilities and only 32% thought that new ideas were readily accepted in their department.[46] Only 19% thought that the public valued their work. Our own survey of government employees in Adelaide and elsewhere confirms these findings.

Down an alley way in Adelaide

Reinventing a bureaucracy: The Adelaide pilot study

In 2014, along with colleague Richard Brecknock, we explored the concept of the creative bureaucracy with state and local government in Adelaide, Australia.

Adelaide has engaged with the idea of the creative city for many years. Charles was a 'thinker in residence' in Adelaide in 2003, itself a programme that exemplified creative thinking. Margie worked for the Adelaide Capital City Committee with a focus on alignment and collaboration between state and local government. The pilot was commissioned by Erma Ranieri, the Commissioner for Public Sector Employment, who was responsible for many reform programmes and who in a previous incarnation had instigated the successful 90 day project outlined above.

The study tested the idea of the creative bureaucracy with internal 'change agents' as well as more broadly with public servants. It summarised the context for creativity for government. It highlighted good examples from across the world. It explored how to better mobilise talent within government, why it matters, and what was preventing the better use of talent and what might spark it more successfully.

Parking day Adelaide requires many agencies to work together

There were more than 20 in-depth interviews with current and former public servants and workshops and discussions with a further group of around 80-100 people. These aimed to unearth the lived experience of working for local or state government. The conclusions of the pilot report were then tested through a survey with 51 responses.

The in depth interviews confirmed that people are highly committed to their work in public service and motivated by making a contribution to the community. Some felt that they had the authority and organizational support to develop their ideas and take them forward. Others felt very frustrated with the way their organization and the system worked. These people could often see the potential – how things could be – but the reality fell far short.

Their frustrations came from a number of directions. Broadly summarised they included management that had little interest in their ideas; other employees within and outside their organization that took a very narrow view of the public servant's role and couldn't think more broadly about possibilities; incompetent or lazy employees that were tolerated and not managed; systems that constrained potential with illogical rules that

made innovation very difficult; over sensitivity to politics and the 'reactions' of politicians or media; obsessions with secrecy, hoarding information and resources; excessive competition with others in the organization or system; short termism and a 'chop and change' approach to policy and initiatives.

For those who had worked for more than ten years the accumulation of experiences could make them more pessimistic about what was possible. But many also developed their own 'philosophy' about work which meant that they created their own projects or adopted codes of behaviour that gave them a sense of control and satisfaction. In doing this they were also likely to find others to connect to in the organization with similar philosophies. Creativity could be discouraged but it would find a way to be expressed for many.

Our follow-up survey showed that 92% thought that creativity was important or very important for the future of the state, the public sector and for them as individuals. But only 51% thought there was a high or very high potential for them to be creative at work.

For places like Adelaide, which is at the sharp end of the transition from manufacturing to the knowledge or creative economy, it's important to mobilise all the resources you have to work with. These cities and regions need to be even more creative than other more successful places if they are to create an identity in the context of the 'noise' created by cities competing for attention. 86% of those surveyed had high or very high agreement that SA and Adelaide needed to be more creative than other places if it was to compete globally.

This is the heart of the paradox. Only organizations already with a culture of creativity are likely to recognise its importance for the work that they do. A culture of creativity within the bureaucracy is likely to create a 'spillover ' effect that can help a city reimagine its assets in imaginative ways. A creative city can't just be an add-on to an unimaginative bureaucracy. It has to flow from an imaginative bureaucracy.

If a city needs to be more creative than other cities to thrive, it needs a bureaucracy that is even more creative again, capable of experimenting around its own processes, leveraging its own talents and taking measured risks.

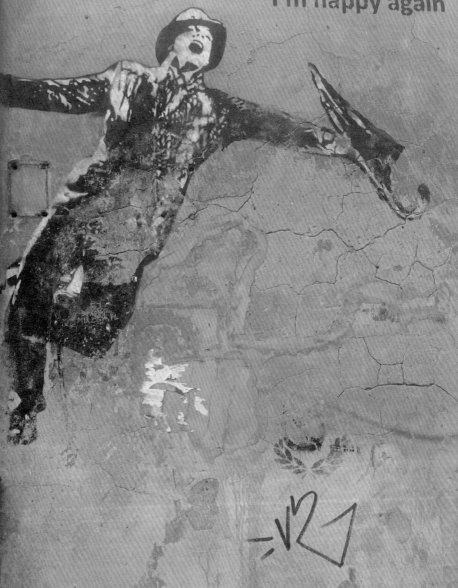

ULICA
BOŻEGO CIAŁA

I'm happy again

RE-ENCHANTING THE BUREAUCRACY

Despite the problems explored here, bureaucracies and the people within them manage to do great work. Some are even quietly heroic – taking measured risks, prepared to deal with the consequences, trying to make a contribution.

The 'lived experience' of bureaucrats is a mixed bag. Much talent is wasted and human potential lost. Others create rich and fulfilling careers and have great impact. But a narrowing of the bureaucratic imagination has real consequences for cities, for society and people.

The bureaucracy will not be shielded from the forces that will automate the routine and repetitive. It will leave the sophisticated and intellectually complex and bureaucrats will only be able to address that effectively if they have been nurtured by an environment that allows for freer thought and action. The public sector is called on to shape the context for great transitions. It also will be required to pick up the pieces where things go wrong.

This is why the culture in the bureaucracy matters. We make no claim that public entities should be creative 24/7, but it is a default position. So much is being demanded of them we need a renewed willingness to listen to its possibilities.

The factors set out below express our sense of what needs to be influenced. These areas are not easy to measure. But we can start to shape questions that might provoke debate and spark new conversations.

Becoming a better bureaucracy

Softening the system

The words 'organization' or 'system' feel cold, hard, rigid and structured. In 'cold' environments people feel closed in. In 'warm' environments they are more active and able to thrive. For a 'cold' environment to 'warm' up it needs to spark human energy rather than reduce it. So much is in the 'texture' of the organization. That is why our focus is on softening the system.

New times and contexts require different skills. In this less deferential age, leaders can no longer be remote and exist at a distance. Nor can they be paternalistic, treating people like children. Their task is to optimize intellectual resources and human potential in pursuit of a mission. This needs emotional intelligence. The dilemma is that emotional intelligence is a nuanced, subtle skill, and harder to teach than technical skills.[47]

Public sector organizations have big missions. But they often lack 'warmth'. They distrust human nature. They see 'hard' controls as essential. Many are yet to see 'employees' as partners in a mission. The tendency is to control and to limit.

Great leaders are capable of dealing with this complexity and ambiguity. They deflect attention rather than demand it. Civic generosity relies on civility in everyday life, including at work. The relationship between bureaucrats and elected leaders is central to success but is continually negotiated and revised as people and 'regimes' change. We need an equality of status between bureaucrats and elected officials. The bigger mission needs to be at the forefront.

... soft skills are the most important in making organizations effective

Mentors may be better than managers. Helping people think is crucial. 'Philosophical mentoring' or counselling is a contemporary movement in practical philosophy to aid clear thinking, has much potential and may grow in importance.

A survey of over 300,000 leaders[48] found that the qualities leaders need are consistent whether one is managing one person or a 1000. Of the top 15 qualities, nine are 'soft' skills, such as: Building relationships, listening, establishing stretch goals, communicating well and building morale. A humane environment inspires people to take the initiative, to give more and to share. Mood is everything. The 'atmosphere' matters.

The philosophy and the structures need to change. According to the authors of 'Creating the Best Workplace on Earth' Rob Goffee and Gareth Jones[49] the best workplaces are 'unusual in their ownership arrangements and ambitions. Many are partnerships, mutual associations, charitable trusts, and social enterprises. Although all share a desire to generate revenue, few are conventional, large-scale capitalist enterprises'. This reminds us of the John Lewis/Waitrose example above.

Warming the mood

Investing in people is also investing in the physical environment. Workplaces have personality. In one you feel human. In another you feel reduced.

Many public sector work environments are better than before, more airy, more open, more congenial. But austerity and lack of resources has left others looking tired, in need of freshening up. In some buildings, deferential thinking is etched into the physical fabric, such as long corridors with closed doors.

The trend toward open plan spaces has, in many areas, shrunk the opportunity for privacy and quiet. Personal space is reducing. In some, fear around security has stripped desktops of personal content along with documents and files.

Office design has psychological impacts. The best help people feel at ease and perform better. The worst shrink people in. The spirit or culture of a place is reflected in the scale, the location or setting and in the small details. Lighting, colour, texture, materials, comfort – all matter. They trigger emotions. Natural wood can feel better than plastic; warm colours can be more relaxing than the shrill; transparency can feel better than being closed in.

Some help you to be more organised, give more of yourself and communicate better. This needs a fine balance between social gathering places, the semi-private to the private. People need quiet spaces for solo work or to switch off. They need spaces to work in a team and to break out. Too open and you lose focus, too closed can isolate you.

The best let in natural light. They have views, greenery, plants, space to stretch and not feel cramped. They reduce distraction and overload and exude more calmness than noise. They allow people to personalize. An office is partly a home from home. A professional atmosphere encourages focus. The office space creates a visual story of what the organization is, where it is going and whether those working there are valued.

The physical environment is rich with symbols. Bureaucrats are adept at reading subtle cues. It's not just the physical design. It's where people are located and the norms that govern behaviour. Teams located close to each other can start to form casual friendship bonds. They collaborate more. Distance may make this harder.

Some locations are closer to 'power and influence' than others. They help bureaucrats be visible to decision makers. Others relegate them to hidden corners where they are rarely noticed.

If locations are too fixed, it fixes the organization mindset too. Being able to move and choose where to work helps people to shift their mindsets and think afresh. Hybrid social/work spaces can free up conversations. They can create opportunities for new combinations.

Engaging the inner self

An engaged employee brings her or his full self to their work. Work should feel important. It should engross, captivate, even fascinate. Work should grab our attention. We then become alert and stretch ourselves.

This process can happen in the 'day to day' of work and in many other ways. Connecting with peers, challenging assignments and opportunities to broaden the mind can build our energy. An atmosphere, routine and 'challenging variety' help us connect the organization's values to our own purpose and meaning. We then invest in the quality and results of our work. We are active contributors.

A bureaucracy that engages with people, within an organization and outwardly across a system, with stakeholders in the community, and citizens is creating the dynamic it needs to face the future.

The relationship needs to be two-way. A person invests in the mission of the organization and an organization invests in the individual as an individual. Creating and maintaining this relationship takes time and, importantly, intent.

> Warm organizations are more fun... They work to bigger missions

When organizations care about people or are kind, they make it safer to take risks. A sense of perspective and humour grows. Warm organizations are more fun. They let off steam. They work to bigger missions. Creative energy helps them 'nut out' ways forward, look ahead, and tackle problems. They endeavour to build up the energy of their people, not deplete it. They see people as individuals and equal partners in a joint endeavour, not according to their level in a hierarchy.

An engaged employee feels and sees evidence that their voice matters. Their individual qualities and strengths are valued. They don't have to conform to a type that sucks out their spirit. They can influence the direction of the organization. They know they will be treated with respect. This does not mean that they will always agree with the choices made. But they will understand why a choice was made.

The values and operating style of the organization is then transformed. The task is to build energy – not leech it of colour or diversity.

*The iconic Holzmarkt
development in Berlin
required bureaucratic
inventiveness*

Relaxing across boundaries

Boundaries are opportunities to see potential, problems and limitations. Boundary crossing is a skilled art and one that a good bureaucracy values and nurtures.

The 'valley of death' between one organization's sphere and another's is one of the greatest frustrations for bureaucrats and citizens alike. It is here in **the 'falling through the gap' syndrome** that the bigger picture and goals of the 'system' get lost.

The 'gaps' between silos need leadership. The challenge is that no one organization can solve the problems nor be credited.

For instance, 'urbanism' requires an interlocking set of skills, cutting across the soft and hard sciences and knowledge. Professional protectiveness can get in the way. Public sector outsourcing makes blending disciplines and insight more difficult. Contracts constrain through specific and tight briefs. Responsibility and accountability can be confused across the public and private sectors. For example, experts in walking, cycling, public transport or cars look at the same issue differently.

Bureaucracies need to frame challenges with ambitions that go beyond typical reporting lines and the goals of the organization. The ambition has to be about something that matters to citizens for the long term.

The places 'in between' can be the most important. To create a 'vibrant place' or 'a city where people are content' or 'make a great street' requires an appreciation of multiple factors – not all of them under the control of one organization. The principles apply across most areas of human endeavour.

Working across boundaries needs a certain type of leadership. It's a leadership that rarely gets credit.

Boundaries are also opportunities for creativity and experimentation. Goals contained within one organization cannot be ambitious enough. But making the most of relaxing across boundaries – the role of the connector comes to the fore.

Connecting the potential

The connector is a vital under-acknowledged skill in city making. It is difficult to become or be a connector in a public bureaucracy. It is a creative activity, often an unseen ability, and can have powerful, catalytic potential.

Successful places have many connectors, both organizations and individuals. **Connectors and facilitators stand above the nitty gritty** of the day to day, important as this is, and look at 'what really matters' and where opportunities lie. By standing above the fray they can focus on bringing people, organizations, ideas and resources together and avoid getting involved in interest group politics. They take an eagle-eye view of things, rove over concerns and see lines of alignment, partnering potential and synergies between supposedly disparate things. They look for the common agenda and highlight issues many view as not of prime importance as it is not their main raison d'etre. This is why being a connector is more than being a networker, although networking is part of the activity.

Cities are **full of opportunities to connect assets in imaginative ways** to create value. Take the biennial solar car race from Darwin to Adelaide. It started in 1987 and in 2015 46 cars from 25 countries travelled the 3000kms on sun energy.[50] The world's foremost solar car race exhibits astonishing forms of inventiveness where universities research labs, high tech companies and enthusiasts come together. The race has been won by Dutch, Swiss, American and Japanese teams over the years. They now arrive in Adelaide in Victoria Square and are admired. But when we last saw them a few years ago, the opportunity to link the teams to the local start-up system, to establish joint projects with the city's advanced manufacturing sector, to hold public lectures or workshops had not been developed. Lessons have since been learnt and now Adelaide is making far more from the connections and opportunities that the race offers.

The connector – person or organization – has a difficult role to play. They need to present themselves as beyond self-interest and be both powerful and not powerful simultaneously. They need authority to draw credible people and organizations together. If they take credit others will be jealous, yet they need authority to operate. The connector needs an unusual set of qualities such as: a clear focus, strategic intent, diplomacy, flexibility, the capacity to read situations and deal with power play; strong conceptual thinking that understands the essence of arguments, capacity to synthesise, to chair and make meetings work.

Cities abound with possibilities that lie under the radar. **Creative connectors are crucial to cities** exploring and experimenting around their existing assets to discover and invent new forms of value.

Bureaucracies are getting better at holding conversations with citizens and are beginning to harness the wisdom of crowds. But many citizens feel a disconnect between being engaged and influencing. It's easy to engage in areas that are less polarised. Some might be seen as gimmicks – others go deeper. Talking differently also needs to happen within and across the bureaucracy.

Drawing on community knowledge and ideas can be satisfying and useful for both bureaucracies and communities. Open platforms make these processes transparent. Many jurisdictions are experimenting with this. For example, the International Budget Partnership gives examples of citizens choosing budget priorities.[51] In other places citizens are invited to help develop legislation. The potential gains are clear - better quality services, revitalized trust and understanding each other better. It goes into the deeper psychological needs or motivations that could create a sense of civic duty.

Unlocking a fresh ideas climate

Day to day organizational life inevitably involves repetitive work, a raft of activities to keep up to date, things to organize. It can be hard to lift the gaze, to question, to learn, and to challenge assumptions. New and urgent challenges from climate change to dealing with diversity cannot be addressed in neat boxes.

Bureaucracies need confidence that being open, curious and democratic will help them to achieve their missions.

They need to ask powerful questions of what will be demanded of them. They need to create a fresh ideas climate capable of supporting these questions. The **tight networks where information is currency no longer works** with the self-organising networks of our era.

The digital world makes it far easier to draw in ideas. It is transforming things at such a speed public bureaucracies must also respond at pace. They will need to be fleet-footed, flexible, far-sighted and willing to experiment.

Strong shifts are transforming most aspects of life. The context for bureaucracies is also transforming. Expectations of what is possible or required may be set too low.

Some cities are asking big questions of themselves. A city that asks how it can eliminate private cars, as Oslo is doing, will be compelled to think about transforming mobility and

*Wall in the Wynwood
Arts District Miami*

the desires of commuters. A city that asks how it can eliminate homelessness as Medicine Hat in Canada has done, will need to transform its role in relation to providing homes.

Seoul's comprehensive anti – gentrification approach will confront developer interests. Climate change will transform what is essential. Freiburg, since Chernobyl in 1986, dared to make solar energy the focus for its development. The point is to break through established ways of solving problems, to the potential for transformation.

'Challenge based' innovation is one way to start. **Bureaucracies can also learn from the start-up culture**. Crowdsourcing ideas, using social media, seeking out 'mavericks' and approaches such as design thinking can open up the possibilities.

'Start-ups' offer techniques that can be easily adopted. Pitch sessions for project and policy ideas can work in public sector settings. Convening experts in a 'brains trust' to build up possibilities rather than pull apart projects need not be limited to Pixar. Conferences and seminars are a traditional route. Commissioning 'experts' to produce challenging 'think pieces' that are then discussed in open forums within the organization is another. Engaging with citizens in various formats from collective scenario setting to trialling prototypes is obvious too. Crucially connecting with interesting bureaucrats in other places and even swapping jobs is not done as often as it should. Finally, of course, drawing in creative ideas from employees.

Constraints, time or resources, can stimulate creativity as it forces you to do things differently. The wider community can help. Think here of the examples of involving the elderly in developing their health programmes. '10 solutions for 21st century healthcare' provides a rich set of examples from across the continents.[52] Consider youth projects where they are more in control such as the German 'Think Big' initiative.[53]

A culture for ideas connects insiders and outsiders in joint missions of discovery and understanding. All those with a stake in the outcome need to be involved from world experts to local thinkers and doers. It can bring the spirit of the festival and the diffusion of networks. Openness can diffuse internal competition and power plays. Ideas can come from many directions.

Rather than picking flaws in ideas to eliminate them, experiments promote measured risk taking by testing hypotheses or ideas out. An experimental culture helps problem solving. Experiments may not need huge investment but they require focus, commitment and attention. They can't be done thoughtlessly. Just the act of experimenting makes organizations and cities feel more interesting. They signal a type of confidence that allows for the unexpected.

A culture for ideas connects insiders and outsiders in a joint mission of discovery

Resetting the culture

The culture of a place brings everything together. It determines the mood, atmosphere, the conditions, the rules and their intent. Is it more 'the letter of the law' or a 'spirit of the law' place? Is it open to interpretation or can people create exceptions? The guiding aim, as mentioned, is to be strategically principled and tactically flexible.

It is alert to the spectrum of 'authority' that can start to treat 'guidelines', internal 'rules' or 'principles' as 'laws'. The connection between rule and intent can be lost. It does not let a 'recommendation' slip into being treated as if it were a 'law'. The reason this can happen is that people want simplicity and avoid nuanced thinking and making a judgement.

Culture is hard to define but viscerally felt as 'the way that things are done around here'. It is the way people treat each other in the system and the way they treat others outside it. It is hard to shift. It can survive a change of government, of leadership and reorganization. It persists even when many people in the organization leave. Culture creates an overarching perspective (more open than closed? more 'yes' than 'no' in attitude?).

People are attracted to work in great cultures. They will do anything to move to a workplace that inspires them, that adds to their energy, frees them and gives them a vehicle to make a difference and solve interesting problems. Great cultures don't have to work hard to attract the skills, competencies and the flair they need. They are magnetic.

Every organization and every city without a great culture has a talent crisis. Everyone wants the best to work with them.

Yet in the bureaucracy culture is often overlooked, taken for granted, assumed to be just the way things have to be.

People will do anything to move to a workplace that inspires them

In the traditional bureaucracy the talented, risk taking and action-oriented people have a problem. They can be disregarded by 'the system' or their department. They can lose resources or authority and even be forced to leave.

Those cities that value and retain talent, are also cities that seem to stand out in world terms. Consider Melbourne, Amsterdam, Ghent – key people have been in their organizations or roles for more than 10 years. They are able to take big ideas and programmes and see them through.

A culture that sees people as replaceable cogs, is more likely to be associated with failure than a culture that recognises the diverse talents of its 'flawed' but real workforce. And being seen as creative has tangible impacts on who applies for a job. Lewisham, the large London borough, for many years had a 'Creative Lewisham' programme. This changed its perception and the quality of staff

Being a better bureaucracy

So far we've explored the factors we believe will be associated with a more creative bureaucracy and why this feels like an inevitable transition.

But with the number one concern of bureaucrats being 'reform fatigue' how will the bureaucracy transition itself? It's not possible to be prescriptive here - so here are some brief scenarios which are not mutually exclusive and can overlap in various combinations.

Scenario 1 – The 'mission-oriented' and bold ambitions of some cities, driven by the fierce challenges they face; the creative ways some cities develop their potential, lead to new models more suited to the times. As these cities forge ahead, translating big ideas into practice, other cities have a 'fear of missing out' and join in. They find their administrations unequal to the task. They increasingly search for new ways of working. It begins to dawn on them that they have been leaking the necessary bureaucratic talent and not making enough of the talent they have. New forms of leadership continue to emerge, far better suited to the spirit of the times. This warms organizations, softens systems, and refreshes the ideas climate.

Scenario 2 – Living laboratories, think tanks, innovation units and other forums for innovation gather pace and demonstrate impact. Cities and governments compete to host and be known for bold experiments. The most interesting of these innovation groups are magnetic, adding power to a city. They are emblematic in the way that major companies or top league universities have been in the 20th century. They attract civic minded people to the big challenges and opportunities – not through a sense of duty - but because they want to experience the energy it brings. This spirit is increasingly embraced across the bureaucracy, partly because it feels essential.

Scenario 3 – A movement of bureaucrats demands better environments, new conditions for working that change bureaucracies from the inside out. An educated, freelance oriented, workforce won't tolerate hierarchical, non collaborative arrangements. As job certainty erodes, people are more interested in making a contribution and honing their skills. There is a merging of citizen led change and bureaucrat led change - it is less distinguishable as to which sector is which.

Scenario 4 – Distracted and fractured cities, regions and nations find it impossible to summon the collective will to take the bold actions necessary to address the inevitable economic, environmental and social disruptions coming from multiple directions. Some places do better and they have the organising capacity and the ethos to get to grips with their culture, their place and grow their own capabilities. It takes more time, but a new model emerges.

Bringing it all together

The landscape of public bureaucracies is vast and diverse. Yet regardless of the culture, place or system – they seem to share certain characteristics.

One is often having a reputation of being slow, difficult and resistant to common sense. Another is being a huge repository of human capital, which is not well used and rarely inspired.

A leadership ethos that enables people to give of their best and a warm organizational atmosphere are the most powerful levers to incentivize 'system' change. From these, motivation, will, ambition and urgency can emerge. These, more than government targets, league tables or benchmarks, can generate the energy to deliver services, deal with crises or create opportunity. This ethos helps keep organizations alive so public value can grow as rarely do bureaucracies die.

Change is inevitable. Now more than ever we need the value that a creative bureaucracy can bring. As we acknowledge, conversations about leadership, management, reform and so on already abound.

But a conversation about the lived experience of bureaucrats, of the conditions that support creative thinking and problem solving, and the conditions that will foster human growth is rare. **The Creative Bureaucracy is a starting point for that conversation.**

Our suggested domains describe the qualities of this more creative bureaucracy. They have emerged from conversations with public officials in Adelaide, Berlin, Helsinki, Taipei, Ghent and Bilbao and are presented here for discussion and elaboration. They build on those generated for the Creative Cities Index, but their focus is different.[54] They assess the public organization rather than the amalgam of individuals, public, private and community organizations that make up a whole city.

Crucially they look at the organization from the inside and how it feels for the people to work there. They also explore how the organization reflects itself in the outside world.

The Domains: Possible questions:

A softer system

Does the organization feel uplifting? How does it help people explore and develop their passions, beyond the work context? Is expressing emotions seen as part of your professionalism? Does the system make you feel at ease or guarded? Are hidden talents assumed to be there and acknowledged? Are softer skills, like empathetic truth telling valued?

A warmer mood

What does the physical space tell you about the culture? What are its key symbols? Is it easy to see who is 'important'? Is the office environment like a 'third space'? Does it feel informal, but focused – organized but not constrained? Do people feel free to organize their own time and to work in places they are comfortable in? Is the organization healthy – is there evidence of substantial sick leave or by contrast people put in an extra effort to make things happen? Is being playful part of normal work life? How would a visitor describe the mood of your organization? Indeed, how are visitors treated?

Engaging the inner self

How do people describe the experience of working in their organization? Do they emphasize the positive or the negative? Is it a story of achieving things? Are they proud to work there? Does the environment look mono-cultural or diverse, such as age, dress or background? Does the emotional climate encourage the better self in you? Is this a place where you love to work that reflects your inner aspirations?

Relaxing across boundaries

How are system wide issues led and supported? Are other organizations seen as competition or as potential allies? Do people take an interest in problems outside their specific area? Is there a sense of a bigger mission beyond the goals of the individual department or organization? What reward is there in noticing and addressing gaps? What lines cannot be crossed? A sense of boundaries is often important and its constraints can trigger creativity, yet is the default position to communicate with others.

Connecting the potential

What are the mechanisms used to help see the bigger patterns and themes inside and outside the organization? Are the resulting conversations rich or curtailed? Are people protective of their ideas or resources or do they share? What happens after meetings? Is the complexity of the connector's role noticed and valued? Are they rewarded? Who gets to be part of the conversation? Is it more open than closed?

Unlocking a fresh ideas climate

What examples are there of bold thinking? Does the organization feel contemporary? Is it possible to challenge assumptions and to reframe issues and even the mission? Is there a good balance between immediacy and what might be important in the future? Where are the ideas debated and exchanged – inside or outside the organization? How much is shared in public?

Resetting the culture

How do people describe the culture? Are rules treated as if they were immutable laws or is their intent seen as most relevant? Are the values human centred? Conflict is inevitable and potentially creative, yet there are people who under-perform. Is the organization able to uncover its sources so it can be managed in the right way? Can the organization deal with difference, those who do not fit the norm or even mavericks? Is it safe to express uncertainty, even at senior levels?

REFERENCES

1 https://www-03.ibm.com/press/us/en/pressrelease/31670.wss

2 Government is Good: http://governmentisgood.com/

3 https://www.oecd.org/governance/observatory-public-sector-innovation/

4 http://mind-lab.dk/en/

5 http://publicsector.sa.gov.au/culture/

6 http://labcd.mx/labforthecity/

7 http://acteursduparisdurable.fr/acteur/urban-lab-paris-and-co

8 http://ash.harvard.edu/

9 https://www.kl.nl/en/

10 http://www.kafkabrigade.org/

11 http://www.nesta.org.uk/

12 http://www.adobe.com/content/dam/acom/en/max/pdfs/AdobeStateofCreate_2016_Report_Final.pdf

13 State of the American Workplace annual series, Gallup

14 http://www.gallup.com/businessjournal/188033/worldwide-employee-engagement-crisis.aspx

15 https://www.psychologytoday.com/blog/theory-knowledge/201405/six-domains-psychological-well-being
and http://midus.wisc.edu/findings/pdfs/830.pdf

16 http://janslaby.com/downloads/slabywueschner_emoagency_draft-2.pdf

17 The Creative City: A Toolkit for Urban Innovators, Charles Landry, 2000, Earthscan, London

18 https://www.nesta.org.uk/sites/default/files/kcfinder/
files/4.1.InnovationinGovernmentOrganizationsPubilcSectorAgenciesandPublicServiceNGOs.pdf

19 Tactical Urbanism: Short term action for long term change, by Mike Lydon and Anthony Garcia, Island Press, 2015

20 http://www.hri.fi/en/

21 https://www.opendemocracy.net/ash-amin/reinventing-democracy

22 http://www.iftf.org/iftf-you/make-the-future/roy-amara-fund/

23 https://www.nytimes.com/2017/02/26/world/canada/homeless-canada-medicine-hat-housing-first.html

24 http://ec.europa.eu/research/innovation-union/index_en.cfm?section=icapital

25 https://en.wikipedia.org/wiki/Hype_cycle

26 http://charleslandry.com/resources-downloads/documents-for-download/emscher-park/

27 https://www.buergerhaushalt.org/sites/default/files/downloads/Studie_Hope_for_democracy_-_25_years_of_
participatory_budgeting_worldwide.pdf

28 http://ec.europa.eu/research/prizes/icapital/index.cfm

29 http://ec.europa.eu/research/prizes/icapital/index.cfm

30 http://calgary.ctvnews.ca/bylaw-bill-set-to-retire-1.898337

31 http://montrealgazette.com/news/local-news/how-calgary-reduced-dog-attacks-without-banning-pit-bulls

32 http://www.dcsi.sa.gov.au/__data/assets/pdf_file/0011/51500/SA-State-of-Wellbeing-Project-Report-2017-02.pdf

33 http://www.openlivinglabs.eu/news/living-labs-guiding-sustainable-cities-innovations-europe

34 http://citiscope.org/story/2014/mexico-city-experimental-think-tank-city-and-its-government

35 http://www.economist.com/node/11701430

36 http://www.hri.fi/en/news/a-transparent-city/

Is this public sector office in Taipei chaotic, creative or does it reveal a convoluted bureaucracy?

37 https://ec.europa.eu/growth/industry/innovation/policy/public-procurement_en

38 http://sydney.edu.au/arts/gsg/downloads/Innovation%20Report_IPAA.pdf

39 http://citiscope.org/story/2014/how-barcelona-and-philadelphia-are-turning-procurement-upside-down

40 http://www.citymart.com/services-index/#our-services

41 http://www.oecd.org/gov/trust-in-government.htm

42 http://www.eupan.eu/files/repository/20160202135959_2016-01-21_-_Public_integrity_and_trust_in_Europe_-_final.pdf

43 https://www-935.ibm.com/services/us/ceo/ceostudy2010/multimedia.html

44 State to Create Study: Global benchmark study on attitudes and beliefs about creativity at work, school and home Adobe 2012 (2016 as well)

45 http://ipma-hr.org/files/GOV13%20BROCHURE%20ADP_V.pdf

46 CSEES_SURVEY_RESULTS.PDF

47 http://www.humanresourcesmba.net/worlds-30-innovative-corporate-human-resources-departments/

48 https://hbr.org/2014/07/the-skills-leaders-need-at-every-level

49 https://hbr.org/2013/05/creating-the-best-workplace-on-earth

50 https://en.wikipedia.org/wiki/World_Solar_Challenge

51 http://www.internationalbudget.org/opening-budgets/citizens-budgets/

52 http://www.innovationunit.org/sites/default/files/DIGITAL%20VERSION%20final%20.pdf

53 https://www.think-big.org/

54 http://charleslandry.com/themes/creative-cities-index/

ACKNOWLEDGEMENTS

Bill Bruce, Erma Ranieri, Margaret Shiu, Jair Lin, Susan Pettifer, Alfonso Cearra Martinez, Idoia Postigo, Richard Brecknock, Thom Aussem, Pieter Ballon, Karl-Filip Coenegrachts, Tim Mares, Aron Hausler, Liesbeth Jansen, Harm-Christian Tolden, Robert Bosch Academy, Jochen Sandig

'A stimulating look at the perennial challenge of how to make bureaucracies simultaneously efficient and predictable, and creative and humane. Helpfully informed by decades of experience its also full of interesting practical examples.'
Geoff Mulgan, Chief Executive, NESTA

'Creative Bureaucracy isn't a contradiction but a force to create positive change. This book delves deeply to explore how we can create, challenge, reimagine and transform our public sector - and why we need to do so now more than ever.'
Erma Ranieri, Commissioner for Public Employment, South Australian Government

THE CIVIC CITY IN A NOMADIC WORLD

A tour de force, this richly illustrated book provides deep insight of where the future city is going and how we can create zones of encounter and places of empathy. Examples from across the world show how citizens and cities are reshaping their urban environment.

'The Civic City is perceptive, important and clearly written.'
Professor Lord Robert Skidelsky

'Utterly timely. Charles uses imagery to tell a powerful story.'
Carol Coletta Senior fellow with the Kresge Foundation

'The visual experience of Charles' book brings the urgent issues facing our cities alive.'
Martin Parr, photographer

nai010.com/en/publicaties/the-civic-city-in-a-nomadic-world-paperback/139143

TITLES IN THE SERIES

All the above titles are all available from: **www.charleslandry.com**